7 Breaths in Yearning

Shaela Montague-Phillips

PublishAmerica
Baltimore

ISBN: 1-4137-6257-3
PUBLISHED BY
PUBLISHAMERICA, LLLP.
www.publishamerica.com
Baltimore

Printed in the United States of America

I dedicate this book to the testament of my soul, to my mother, Alecia, and other family members who believed in the power of my words and challenged me not to accept my fate but to conquer it and make it my own.

Table of Contents

A Song of a Woman

Today, I saw a woman beaten
She reminded me of myself, after the war
Where deferred dreams come easy
Tattered from her beloved;
un-kissed, who knows hard licks
that don't stop in the middle of trying
Finding hope in the crevices of fingertips

We are the same woman,
now after I un-stripped the paint
The pigment, the identity from *"us,"* creatures
--I lurk in shadows, double featured

I am that woman whose spirit can't fit her body
Damned in heaving a soul one piece at a time
Tired of counting pennies, lifting cushions
Feeding a heavy chin…*"I am want more than this"*
I shun mirrors all with my pinkie,
we paint skies fluorescent

Sometimes, I have trouble trusting
I found a piece of peace in my pocket;
--folded in a crunch-knuckle-bound
It was lost in my harvest;
entwined with lapped roots.

I am swollen from the years that don't pay good enough
My resilience has been pushed in waiting
The door once stopped moving;
and I am propaganda's herstory
Painted in silent dress

Whip lashed, *the full intensity;*
where revolution combines in civil war
Dividing-personalities
unable to find its tempo
We share the same tongue;
to exist

I am trading places, developing
Hushed held-back, still
Withered in wants
These days I know someone is always watching, *looking*

In the meat of my woman flesh
My tears crumble down to the curbs of my shoulders
Following the dreams and wishes, "*I could have had*"
Before war lashed my destiny

Birth

her smooth lush womb flowing spills gently
goosh-it was mama that heaved me
pushing past moon's equinox
though, exerted she cries
hungry held ripples
as she launches
taunt exhale
sings my
birth

Daughter

if i were born in the 70s, i would have been
a revolutionary baby, high fists shouting for black power,
sportin' cat eye glasses in pick-me afros, never to add-in a perm
i feel the airstreams stale creased in my eyelids,
sublimed messages, *america trying to tame my mind*,
i am at the border checking lice in dreams

i am ready to enter the grace-lands of america,
the cadence adventure echoing in ruined mucks
past brownstones, corner shops hanging carcasses
stenches of drained meat, paralyzing my nostrils
upward in mobility of small mom-and-pop stores,
still existing to suck what's left out corporate america
all over the *Hill*

i am led by light-stashed-smog up against the city
words-fall-asleep-in-the-wind-tapped, in angry pits
then, as if, my name, unhindered-*nonexistent*
i am stuck force feed in an open world pushed
through reality, reformed in between rushing cars
i pause--

on PAT buses we Pittsburghers rush to find a seat, relax
shoulders tense away from sun-warmth lingering
"We don't even know who are our leaders are any more"
two older women marinated in Ben-Gay speak loosely

time warps,
in between the rally sessions at the Urban League pulling
together secret meetings on how to vote, *if you're black*
we are collected by our city from lax people slow to
see the city change; i am coated with equal signs,
puzzled in fragments, torn wishing to be invisible
amidst bare junctions, empty handed, here passing
flyers-*for what I believe in*, came out of mounds,
where the clock ticks away my possibilities

rushed in debris of empty tomorrows, while
i am standing on floors where sit-ins happen,
and the Honorable Martin Luther King gave his speech,
i realize my cry is only a soft murmur calling for a
change-*i can't always hold the rain, suck dry fate,*
restore, let my fingertips be like magic wands

i quench my thirst in iambic bows contorted,
rooted in the dusty core, be re-titled,
the daughter of America,
i am fuming in resentment,
locked in bottoms of shackles,
left by father not knowing ME,
trying to find out who i am,
the *dream-seeker, soul searcher*
trudging

trading places, where the peace has a long-standing
mockery, blemished in sunken shoving crowds,
drugged out mothers hiding crack in-between their titties,
chalk lines cradling corpses never to wash out the sidewalks

i live in a redefined America
where there is a suspect on every corner,
children play in stolen shopping carts,
consuming ramen noodles every day of the week
calling women bitches,
throwing rocks at buses,
to savvy their way into another statistic
another ghetto-gangsta budding from the concrete

we hide in fear of being associated,
we don't talk to cops in doorways,
we stand puffing on cigarettes
looking for action in-between blinds
we are immune to the shots,
and the politicians knocking
wanting our vote to win the election.

Beautiful Belinda

i sit in between your legs
while you braid patterns in my hair
slightly tilted, wobbled even,
you brushed, then greased my hair,
you held the hem of my ends,
while soothing my part
your wrists get tired,
while rocking rows in rhythm
the rounded bees are undone
sorted bare hand
my hair grew long,
your crossed legs, *practiced*
conditioned to the sleep of my heavy head
the silver foil would hold the beads in

smiling for my preschool picture
i was beautiful
my schoolboy glasses
pushed on the bridge of my nose
tucking my lip in, teeth out
i gave the picture of a lifetime

while resuming a straight course on Sunday,
you crossed the jordan river,
had conversations sipping pop,
ironing our clothes,
hands on hip,
dinner that hummed at our souls,
you taught me how to be a lady

Secret Oath

At the playground
we shaved color off of skin
And became pirates of the monkey bars

We cut kitties out of paper,
Writing names
behind the school,
using black markers

Our oath in chalk,
we swore to memorize
under slides that became our castle,
after the popular girls became prissy
and forgot its existence
our badge of honor,
was skinned knees and
rust on the seams
where our jeans hugged hips

we saw in our mind's eye,
and envisioned famous people
out of clouds
best friends that wonder,
lurking in the grass

plastic trumpets,
we marched high-step
down the streets
playing for pennies,
swinging on trees
into the never-lands

Summer Sizzle

the
slick scorching sun
sing praises
to us girls in
halter-tops and pedal pushers
selling
icies
50 cent
a cup

we were
working
girls
making lemonade
too sweet

advertising different
posted flyers
on tree trunks
flavors that made
people beg for more
on a sugar-high
they would suck the juice out

two locations,
we had a double window swinging service
working ma-ma,
when we were skipping buses
sitting by droopy draw men, funky

to the east hills shopping center
shoving dollars in jars
splitting quarters for the candy store
behind the buildings,
we would play double-dutch
and sing the new songs from radio

For Easter

my mother,
would scare straight beaded curls
below my neckline
with a heated hot comb
greasing crevices with Blue Magic

all for Easter

my powdered blue dress,
with the white lace
down the center
was set across my bed
and my velvet black shoes
sat and waited for a princess

I wrote letters to God,
on a chalkboard near my pillow
repenting my sins
placing the gold rimmed garnets in my ear
i was perfect
Anyone need a model for Sears?
placing on my gloves
i walked down the stairs
like a princess
it was time to go to church

Daisy Hippies of the New World

our feisty fingers grabbed flowers out of people's yards,
daisy hippies of the new world, the pansies were jealous
shriveled in their domain and their vortex ate our hands,
their evil grins put on skirts, becoming mamma chicks
and died on spot

but that did not stop us

our thievery was brilliant, dancing, snatching, later
offering it to the ground, we had a burial for the earth,
that wept for its snatched children, we strolled
into fenced patios under delphinium skies

our eyes opened, we saw hues, petals screaming to be
taken into hair skipping on blue plastic bows the
streamers off our bikes flicking, *fast--*
perfect in bursting are the roses
in a parade, so pronounced to *garden*-shoplifting

we suffer from being collectomaniacs at a young age

the world spins around, thinking quick on its axis,
we pick the best, a headband in our hair, *there are yellows,*
with tints of violet embers, twisting a contorted,
epileptic-palette into a splendiferous vibration.
grabbing thumb-*fulls,* as nature's soil delivers a
renewal to its petals, now swaying a braided in the
learning rod open wind upon an earthen watercolor.

Roses in the Rain

my memories are fading fast
in the pamper box
we would throw our blocks while drinking milk

we kept the outside out
under the table
crawling fast in between things
we are like brother and sister
play tag
hit
kiss hug
our childhood happy

Sitting out in the driveway making mud pies,
counting rain drizzling in the sky
Finding yellow rocks,
it must be gold,
We would play in the trees, under the left arm,
And spill our red containers full of jumping beans,
while running in the yard

playing hide-and-seek
you have to find me first

Digging in grass to pull red roses
From the roots,
we would drop button candy to grow them back,
making the roses sweeter
Leaving our earthly present on the kitchen table,
We would ride our big wheels on top of the rainbow

Rosy Reminiscences
--Dedicated to Grandma

She laminated her age in an oval frame
When her cascade of youth was plentiful in color
She saw pigtails and *hand-me-down* dresses
Hair fastened with plastic rose clips

She wanted her summers back,
The smell of her children eating
rice pudding in yesterday's container
messy twins with milk mustaches
and tired feet victim to crayons and paper

Looking at years ago from the window
The silver wire hangers on metal bars in closets
Rusted, *now,* the chairs sit in formation
for five children, rest empty

In small places there are hints of chalice pathways,
Transparent in the clouds, draped in layers of the stars
Blues walls remember chalk hopscotch on rainy days,
and quite reading in the attic

Scooped in arms full, are the memories
High places in a parachute
Gliding down for the sprouts to hold on to
Polished-packaged recollections

Weight of Dust

undercover diva
just now opening-my-soul
pushing through thick skin
i contain many bodies
harvesting empty husks,
cruelty of my genes

i was raised to be a feminist,
on the summit hills of evolution
wrestle free or live, the urban
empty streets, vacated drums
silent tapping at the skulls
to waken

i can touch-lands with my tongue,
the ones i was promised as a little girl
on origami wings, paper-mâché clouds, gliding
catch me if you dare-the car alarms tweak,
the row houses stretching beyond the end
this is my obtuse horizon

my reality is a fire-*leading the escape*
caught by the claws
I choke on the cataleptic breath
humming on jack hammers
and white men invading my dwellings
foreigners to our parameter, **we measure**

the weight of dust

Fallen Rivers Broken

Fallen rivers broken, changed course in direction
Slivering in lift lids in the banks and through the reservoir
I will never forget the day I met my friend in our meeting room

At 6, we hugged, playing transformers and dolls
Leaving my trust that I would see him again,
Him and his dad, with my step-dad and me

In the apartment lavish curtains
He bragged that his daddy was taking him to a trip to McDonald's
And after following the trails they would go hunting in Frick Park

He only left his son for a minute,
what parents say when they lose their children
to get bullets out his trunk

his son in the woods
where a killer sat watching his prey suck on French fries
eating cheeseburgers
Sipping orange pop
Playing with his new toy freshly out the Happy Meal box.

I listened, watching
a body in the trees was found this morning
Covered in his urine behind the tracks

The news anchor does a close up of his little brown hand

And the picture switches, showing a six-year-old boy
Brown eyes, snaggletooth, smiling for his pictures

And with out pausing, one, breath,
"Is that Michael" asking my step-dad
He nodding in disbelief his jaw hanging below,
he dials his best-friend's number, but the phone was busy.

Halfway to Oblivion

Don't forget the toilet paper, and here is
2.40 for a stick of butter

I was almost halfway to oblivion
when ma asked me to go to the store
Moist lips grip on dehydrated boots
On sandy rocks on the limbs of fields
Walking, chasing obsessions clinched in blur
I want to board ships that slowly soar down
Return, go back to the spring only if I had too
My ma paid me fifty cent just to go,
i had plans 'wit that money
gonna get me some lick-a-maid

Piggy tails with red bows on Park Hill Drive
Crusty knees walking
Unfamiliar girl walking in somebody's yard
While they lick icies in my face
And get wet in front of the fire hydrogen on Bracey

Packed streets with girls and boys
Most in my class
I look
Parched lip, smiles

"You the mail lady's daughter, ain't you"
"Yup, that's my ma" I say

we splash in the water just a lil'
until 15 minutes go past and up in the parking lot at Zane's
my tenna-shoes squeaking

jean shorts
have the imprints of my Saturday panties
past the cherry tree, breaking branches
skipping fences, swinging in cargo
slamming gates, up the hill

I opened the door to my house
and forgot everything

In Conventional Loving

mincing garlic
i pressed memory
when fresh wind
assumed direction
blossom trees frozen
for next spring

yield

it was the house
pass tearing spaces
pumpkin demons lured girls
into feel good naughty
turning them into groupies

they called only the best back

i became a woman over night
not even wearing chanel no. 5
our bodies overlapping
stretched down in full length
jeans and socks touch disappearing trains

he wasn't gentle anymore

the compression of his body
weighing over our two toned skin

no

he ate me with his eyes
minuscule under his slow chill
his machete sliced in holes
whispering in my ear
i love you

but whores can't love

thinking that would do the trick
he continued holding me down
licking my earlobe
and i
would not discover my song
until 10 years later mincing garlic
un-caged, undelivered
learning how to love again

stop

wobbled dip-side novice
position packed in
the crescendo vibrating in my panties
i closed my eyes and forgot
turning tables
skipping rhythms
dangled quiet melodies in time

Carted Stories

my aunts cart stories in their purses,
they rent memories back for popular demand,
we children know them by heart

singing oldies till the moon lights the sky
while grandma shakes her shimmy
meeting the brightest star

we will past the memories of foliage
to our unborn children
when bellies are full

laugh,

our jubilees can ship time into space
traditions stay the same

our remember whens,
will become myths

envisioning he-man and she-ra
gliding downstairs, chipping teeth

tag in the dark until some one cries,
cousins like brothers,
slicing basements into realms
of the unknown magic
until our eyes catch up with our bodies
slipping into sleep

Beautiful Girls

why can't I be beautiful like the girls in my school
the ones that sit behind me and pluck the back of
my neck, they never have to struggle with their
weight and have been exquisite since the day school started.

they wear the latest fashion, always with fringes
and pleats neatly tucked, braids that hit the center
of their waist, they dance like hip-hop fly girls
too young to interview on *Living Color*
they sing songs from Al B. Sure while
snaking their bodies

playing hand games I would eavesdrop and practice
until I could hopscotch good enough to be invited in
I would tie two ropes to the doors, circle, circle
double-dutch until they noticed, if I had a voice
I would have told them my deepest knowledge

I suffer from being neurotic, a slice of the peripheral
at an early age.

Discolored Places

I.

the smell of spaghetti sauce hits my nose,
warm grits and hog maws roasting like fine spun silk,
all enclosed in this yellow building,
discolored in mixed dust levitated, then deflated,
when the doors slam shut no one can get outta here

the maintenance men only overlaps the brown paint
once a year to cover the smog filled walls,
but even that can't wash out the stale fog
arched in our passageway
i-close my eyes and wish it all away

honey brown bar had another shooting,
ms. gloria busty eyed, voluptuous, saw everything,
the scrapped-up shot glass, the clean sweep--
the cops leave no trace, no evidence that anything
ever happened, *seconds pass*

the news hits my building like a piece of paper on fire
quick-quick, the washed chalk lines persistent
embroider the side walk, the only time the streets
around these parts show some color...

II.

the courtyard where my friends and i made cardboard
box-tree houses, on the cement grounds were kicked
down by disgruntle neighbors, *that could not respect our imagination*

we wished-*hard*, we found a place where trees
bloomed over the thick fences to keep us in.

we got penny candy from Green's store
up the hill, on the corner between
Hamilton and Brushton Avenue
our ponytails fanned out, biker shorts
that skimmed up our knees, inspired by our youth

our unknown origins inspired us to live who we were
we played 7/11 in high grasses behind El Court,
where everyone knew us by name
we painted fingernails and jumped hopscotch
only to leave our marks too…

my home-place can be seen from the spit shine boots
when I get dressed just to go downtown
away from welfare lines,
sun-crumbs that were never promised
to ever be anything more, but, the ghetto
not in me-just influenced, pushed like a nasty taste
flung on my lungs and lasting here in this place

III.

i can recall our skips on sullied quests exposing our arrivals,
wondering in openings, where light isn't present, there,
we could not pop the bubbles that kept us in refuge
we capped our minds mechanically, *no one had to tell us*

the windows like barb wire, hits my wrist leaving imprints
i imagine myself stuck behind here…**forever**
chained like my ancestors, exchanged from plantation to ghetto

never finding a pink opening

will i be the woman who still believes i can sweep
myself to a different place, *or be trapped*
under a carpet lifted in secret, bags of dimes
rolled under the top of my stalkings
the air full of steel-blue tucked in the straps of my bra

something has gotta be better than this

the nights where mama held us under her belly
while the mice played patty-cake in our living room
i erase the urban out my mind, scared straight to
never pass it to my children

the memories or shadows still angled in warm breezes
away from us chocolate know-nothings that run free
the haze transformed close but we watch, *always*
never loosely open doesn't exist, forget, brainwashed,
until *home-wood* is a distant line on our tail bones.

Panthers Back as Women

my mama meowed in the night
had flavor
no errors on flesh
she elongated claws of love
held her young close
with her magic paws
she cooked pot of stew
off last monday's dinner
we children hang in the balance

drinking from our sippy-cups
danzled by her strength
chin up mama
when the day is long
you meowed commands
and braided your hair in two parts
one line straight down the middle
yellow halter tops
we sleep on water beds
eating grilled cheese sandwiches
while watching Star Search

and 106 Jamz plays "We are the World"
it was my favorite
to have my body stuck between
the mahogany boards
to fill your warmth

our smiles identical on black carpet daze
it was a nightmare to have the continual
dream of falling down the stairs

we lost our place
my home since birth
I knew where everything was put
all my adventures started there

in the middle of the jungle I am fending for my own
I learned how to purr from my mama
to pull my strength from the back of my throat
and screech in the middle of the jungle.

Indigo Womb

I had a voice, *once*
The woman in me burned, *I swear*
Sweet aura muted-seized, *until my coming out day is re-announced*
My coals burned on my soul heavy

My hair auburn repressed from the slick-backs
And gum-band ponytails where the sun's arrival
Is aching for attention, the season's signature
Is rippled with skid marks of déjà vu

Quiet in little girl memories, interrupted
I was left behind when I couldn't move on
When mama's mountain slung with rocks in cheeks
I left to pick up pieces,
my little sister and I ready to win the war at 8

At 8 I saw too much, mama with her company
And smell that reeked in my house
The pipes and smoke, cough-*asthma*
I spoke to my baby dolls and repeated,

One time I picked up the receiver, pushed 9
But 1-1 didn't come after, because she was mommy--
my wonder-woman and maybe if I packed me clothes
Went back to daddy, she would stop
And I could have my house, again

The quiet secure space, the chapters that I left
The childhood I lost when I became a woman
And the fingers that peeped in my room while
everyone was high, ssssshhhhh, I slip the quilt
over mama's knees, I am taking over,
the door shuts, in the hallway, I cry~

Lady in a Blue Dress, Worn

Such a lady
With black curled tips
Soft mahogany skin
The woman I always wanted to be
Become the open shell, shining
Moving my fingers
Dangling earrings
Put on makeup
Just like her

She wore a cashmere
powdered blue dress
Stunning, I smell sweet
perfume depicting sounds
Fringing, iron
Buckled blue suede shoes
Lipsticks broken
Loaded up pins

Here-is her freedom
in the back pocketbooks
Cropped-it was the permanent
last breaths, before
She walked out the door
Us in our nightshirts

Complex, but we understood
We cradled hollow dreams
Fingers webbed in nibbles
Plucked by- *be goods*
momma might meet someone new
worthy to *her*-love *us*

The shatter of dead end nights cabarets
When we were left woven waiting, like
Cold ribs from *I-wanna-dance-kisses*
Crystal candy lollipops on pillows
enveloped in plastic dreams, *scattered*

Potato salad wrapped, *save half for your sister*
We watched, I remember
Beneath still mourns

My Daddy's Gun

when, i was younger
my father's gun sat on top of the cabinet
obsolete from the world
he would only shoot twice,
new year's,
open deer season,
when his eye's got bloodshot
rummed up, coked up, **rage**

we kept that quiet hidden from the world
in the secret shame of the Montague's on McConnell Rd,
outstretch in the white-sided country home, back road
he would clean his burgundy barrel chess piece,
metal beauty caressing her like his wife
dance with her gutters, clean out the splattered blood
and rest her, there, folded in the white cloth
she could do no wrong

his inability to love us children, properly
could be blamed for the many nights
he stood, becoming good ol' army boy
slurping deer stew with rutabaga,
ox tails and corn muffins on the side
his, lovely lady sitting on his knee
with the rigid yellow cotton, cleaning
on grandma's kitchen table

my yankee skin curled
on these vacations away from stability
when my practiced prayers were said,
performed, for every blue moon's daddy
i would take the hex out my body
three times removed
and be the perfect daughter.
get everything right, while we stood
in ends watching
eating slender chocolate cake
sipping half-full sodas, we saved after dinner

taped sesame street, was postponed once more
'cause daddy took out his gun
giggling, we sat admiring our personal idol
looking at the bronzed god, GI Joe Daddy
to us, he could do no wrong
we forgot his M-I-A status
when mama called begging

1994

we took a picture up against the fence
biker shorts and osh pokosh jeans
classic2halfage
field open we framed our youth
hit a button right into our memories

ring pops and blue tongues
fists of-*grab it while we can,*
before we get too old to remember
fast alleyway girls and big boys on bikes
they make our butterfly panties hummmmmm

our lipstick too rosy
eyeliner chasing rainbows-*never-ending*
we fell into love on our soft palms
some left with babies
others scarred with damper questions
scared straight- *those will be the ones never to return*

we made copies of our picture
with our fanned hair-dos
budapest angels of the twentieth century
clustered in a ray of sugar babies
sucked hard breath

they found my friend's mother at the
bottom of the river that year
autumn was coming close and the smell
of the honey dew crept into our windows
cold chill too much to ever go

back to being innocent
across the overpass
below the new/pails of charcoal
laid the secrets/welfare slaves
rocked back offspring of 1994
our overalls hung low like the
prison stories the older kids told us
that's when red cursed and blue ruled the blocks
we were spinning into lust with those on house arrest
our only plan, was survival~

That Summer

the july sticky sun hit our backs
as the grass scratched our high thigh
that summer, *i became a young woman*
my cycle of life began and it was then
that i got my first training bra
it was tan with blue and yellow butterflies
they were printed in little patterns
and i wore it every day,

i had been waiting 1 year and 5 months
for my chest to grow with my body
my best-friend had a bra
a boyfriend already,
she had been kissed before i was
and when she played hopscotch
she would tilt her shirt for
all the neighborhood boys to see

this year it would be me
i could now jump double-dutch
and clench my breast
as I "willed" in the air
the young girls would chant:
"police lady
police lady
do-yah
do-yah
'cos here come the lady

we would jump rope in the hot sun
that summer
i would break away from my ponytails
every little girl's trademark
and dye the front of my bangs blonde
parting it on the side with a touch of curl
i was fresh and i knew it
us girls would sit on steps
painting our nails with yellows,
reds, and greens
every day we would play 7/11

we wanted to be caught and mangled
in 7 kisses and 11 pumps
we would venture farther
away from our streets
into the distant jungles of homewood
i was curious, *then*
too curious for my own good, *then*
and i knew it

i wanted second base,
but third base was for bad girls
and i wasn't that
instead I settled for the first time
i had friends that knocked

on my door and called me
it was the first summer the boys
saw me and wanted me ...
so I gave in
that summer

Scattered

your angelic beauty swift with care
has bared too much
harden with all that you are given
still you keep trucking
never looking back
never not once stopping
not for me or us
not for all those roadblocks
that has damned your way

or the misfortunes that have
tortured your very soul
you keep trucking, *mamma*
keep caring
keep loving, *mamma*

my ladybug of faith
hands harden with ash
yet your true love shines through
on scanty means we drunk sleepy time tea
putting it in your pocket
remember mama,
when you called grand-dad
to set rat traps on 536 Brushton Avenue?
he said if they took one bite
they would dissolve just like that

on Saturdays, my covered sister's buggy
filled with clothes

from the wondrous old place
we took one bag at time
it reminded us of how sharp we use to look,
we savored the moment

laundry bags filled with yesteryear's clothing
while walking to the mom and pop's shop
and your face so determined with baby girl on hip
while I walked behind trying to hold on the box of Tide
slightly -spilling its particles on my tee shirt

on the side step,
i chewed on sunflower seeds
admiring the high school girls with their fanned ponytails
with bangs dyed blonde at the center
i remember you hugging me
loving me softly, 'cos i am your first
while our baby was curled up in the stroller

under her favorite pink blanket
we sat folding white sheets as the sun sets
we were a closer family then
poor, but a little rich family
needing each others' love to get us through
this storm

Holding In

August sun zoomed across my head as it yawns, *"Wake Up!"*
And I on the lower bunk awake to a staring eye
I bend upward and step-dad visions me like mother
Playfully pushing me on top of his lap
His arms rope around me, revolved in a pattern
As he slipped his slim legs in-between
Rocked back in forth like I was stepping in double-dutch ropes

It was fun at first,
I was the cowgirl and very early
Should I tell
        No I won't tell
I was shown how to ride the pony
He touched me
And searched me
if I opened my mouth,
two families would have been in pain
my sister got hurt, and that too was all my fault
let mama tell it

The times that I could have taken her to school
Or brought her to the corner store with me
And I couldn't not tell for me, *not for her*
Her four-year-old voice was smaller than mine
And I didn't know how to be a big sister, *then*
To protect her
To be her hero
Because I loved him,
he was more than father was
And I needed that

My childhood smiles were
interrupted into big girl grins
That sinned
I was quiet
Because I loved him,
I was willing to forget
His betrayal to my body/mama's body
He was the monster that crept
under my sheets/ mama's sheets at night
That silenced my feeling to fight
And crept in my mother's bed at midnight
Where was peter-pan and wendy
To wisp me a way to never-never land
To remove my cupped hands from my eyes to see

My mother deserved someone to love
So I forgot, *for her*
Silencing myself I wanted a perfect family
One with mommy
and Daddy
and baby sister

Weapons were concealed in our house, *so we thought*
But little did they know there was one was in our very house

A Silent Effect

My stepmother called me
a product of lust,
I find myself remembering
the exact words she said,
I am that girl trapped
with empty feelings
muted, from never fighting
her lingering phrases,
instead, I see pictures
ones that have empty spaces
without me

my gravitation has coal tips
in the soles, trying to elbow
my way in their unfilled home
yank, reclaim my title
give the illusion that everything
will be all right, *'cos i don't*
want to be my father
lost-lonely, screaming for someone
to hold my spirit

giving my essence to everyone
who listens, *hard-luck* primed
stripped of love from never
being created in it, sore spot
trying to heal on diabetic wounds
instead, i want to paint my soft spirit
in pink, with answers to questions
my family dares not to ask

replies that unveil the eyes of me
my simultaneous combustion
rooted, for confrontations
wanting to sizzle cigarettes
in their foreheads long enough
to remember my 16-year-old
fortitude, before she uttered
those words that still echo
their presence in my mind.

Throwaway Kids

We were throwaway kids
flipped in the wind storm
swept up by carbon paper,
licked by lizards in restless hands
careless loved lies in dirty cameos
the ungloved hands filled no-no's

in the ward of the state,
we dis-inherited our chances to marry into
rich homes embraced with legalized sin
we picked up our brown bags,
and became He-man and She-Ra in a new world
locked, twisted lips on broken smiles, but we smile
bitterly, the best faith was from the shelter
when the jeans were rotated Monday-Wednesday
jogging pants in between

we forgot this all

we are thrown into not knowing
on top of floating spirits inside,
hungry for the fire that once shot messages
when we returned-hell was un-buttoned
waiting to dig in our pockets
and spend our loose change

trying to claim our souls, are you?

but we saw the promise land
the north star, on road maps displayed.

Without Hit

manipulation over matter
she had done what was asked
a boundary shattered
after she had vacuumed,
hung laundry,
five steps from the door
luggage thrown together
boarded bus

and kissed life good-bye
walking to the nearest shelter
she founded freedom
her bare stomach,
parch throat raw,
from the dictation of her husband
seizing control bravely
she wept

her daughter speaking endless dialogue,
chattering at her desperate intuition,
incarcerated pure love,
tainted by broken vessels,
twice aloof,
would never return

that was not home

viscous fluids that write marginalia
split between her pants

she dreamed
of her singing
a better life
one without hit
so she walked tucking images under her arm
to a life without him

My Soul Given

my mama told me that when you lay down
with a man you give him your soul
he takes your essence and that's why
women are so attached--

I am a victim of havin' given my soul
to too many wrong men, assumed by
the grips of wanting to find love
absolute by the sensation of felt-careful
hands, *this is all I ever wanted*

no longer do I turn men's heads the way I use too,
storing away my memories-*a soup pot*, I
stir, long black boots and shirts that dip
below my cleavage. My only accomplishment
is a blown horn or a hard stare-*with Damn Baby*

heavy gold chains brush nipples with one thrust,
one week after we talk on the phone for hours at a time
I wonder why my decision is to lay my spirit
over easy ladled in-*will you ever call me again?*
his grip all over this lost daughter
I get drunk of his passion, *his kiss*

my soul passed as many times as
I have given my telephone number
from the moment I found where my apple bottom
had a core, its been eaten, consumed and thrown away

Safety V

i paid to sip the sun serving in bonnets,
pink skinny-minis, filled to the top
mustard skies diluted with ketchup
on the curvature of bellies
my fertility of youthfulness
on thin filaments of stars
in cotton ribbon bows, running, ragged,
pedaling against the air,
huddling in shadows up against
stone walls seeking badness

concealing fame in gravity,
till the bottom of my heels
negotiated with streetlights,
i bleed drinking hiccups
uprooting reverberations,
quoting dares in thickly coats
of blush wiping before home
shifting gears saying goodbye
to the older working girls that
took their job way too seriously

i was a volunteer never looking
them in their face across
the road where the drunks
acknowledge their sippy-cup
deities crashed on pavements,
walking around them to get
candy for full payment from management,
in those hip huggers, I bought with my allowance

i knew i had to play it cool
down those rosy cheeks
not surrendering to the sword
double dipping in the bends
before time hit my cheeks

against the lovely-hood of promises
in all the wrong places, tootsie pop
womb to protect me, climbing into
my safety v, the bomb shelter closing
the lid below my belly button
waiting until the tornado is done

Sister

It's hard to believe that she is no longer
the baby with soft smooth skin, and that
toothless smile, she left her pink blanket to
embrace her thumb, her two front teeth are rounded
her coarse brown hair falls past her neck
she no longer needs me to point out words
and read her Grimm's Fairy Tales at night

Every morning at 7:45 while my sister and I are sleep
my mother goes off to work, my sister wakes up
very quietly and turns it to the Cartoon Network
and hides the remote control watching dull-colored reruns
I battle to watch the television, she goes outside to play
I hear the way she talks to her friends making
them sound like gods always compromising, sometimes allowing
her friends to go first in double-dutch

I am always protecting her, **always**
it's now her turn to jump in-between the circling ropes
her hair moves back and forth
along with her delicate body,
I hear the way she talks to me,
making me fall under a spell
I watch her from a distance

It's an honest day's work to kiss the wounds of a 7-year-old
to rub the beaded strand of tears off her face
to boost her confidence, "Next time you'll be faster."
I miss when she needed me, when she depended on me

I love the way she holds me now just expecting me
to protect her from all that could and would ever hurt her
realizing after all that she is no longer the baby that i once knew

Uncovered
—for Uncle Bunny

Uncovered manuscripts of uncle's writings,
Newsletters, and binders filled with
musty browned paper
That's how I discovered it,
The art of poetry

My eyes gazed at words
sounds that filled my mouth
It was those words that stumbled
and jumbled in me
Falling in to a rhythmic freestyle
with a hint of '60s revolution

It was the first time that I could
hear myself clearly and loudly,
stepping in to the realm of poetry
My actions weren't mine, but given
for another line of poetry

I studied me, the walk of me,
the soul of me,

and the realization came to me

that before I am anything,
I am a poet
Caught in dreams' dwelling as time capsules afloat,
for I am poet's past and poet's future

then my 12-year-old voice came alive!

In the Girls' Room

in the girls' room
the smell of magic markers-hiccup gossip,
that too became my therapist
hard knocks on salty licks
bloody noses fear-laughter
slurping away at my uneasy spirit

far-too close away
stood still on time, illusions
laziness in bathrooms
where i hide me, my soul
booths where i heard girlie chatter
lip stick smacks
smoke clouds, fluorescent above me,
where pads and toilet paper coded walls
occasional throw ups, *girls with more problems than me*

water paved down hair
tip fingers, wiped stain eyes
are you ready to go,

i console myself in the smudged up mirror

smile-*Shae*
the pink eye raw fused in broken rainbows
no equation could ever understand,
this mountain of poisoned breath
when the crisp fall leaves
became underfoot snows

breezes of quick run home
like a ghost walker,
testament to a revelation
writing scriptures quick to come,
palms of cold ink rushing,
splattering its jaws
on hydraulic formulas relentless like rain

in the girls' room
i sat blindly at the orbits
cries of dreams
brittle on this pale face
i closed the bridge
understand

We Manage

i was told today my mother was pregnant,
on the eve that i arrived meeting my father for the first time,
500 miles where comfort was advancing then ending,
my change fusing then erupting, once i fast forward
my limits in a new region meet everyone with open arms,
whisper back-talks, the brags of my half-sister too obvious,
it made me jealous she went to Walt Disney World twice,
while i was stuck in Pittsburgh-she playfully extracted
my knowledge on how good of a life I was living

i was the daughter that he didn't want,
the curve ball the one he could say he spat out,
i had to beg him to *love me still for nothing at all,*
he gave me issues on how to pose,
like i am really happy in this life,
my mind running, a crash course
in fatherly advice in a week,
he was a monster to me on strips of film
on the quench of demands,
i wonder what life could have been like if i traded spaces

he said, later, if he could will his wallet to
bring me back to Carolina in the same sentence
i brought myself to see him convincing
myself that my love, if thrown could
give him something to think about.
if i told him how much we struggled with
$25.00 a week, may be he would cut
open his vein and want me to have
everything my sisters had.

we manage, us, my mother, we stand,
i asked my mother years later:
why didn't you ever petition more child support,
why didn't you make him pay to care?
we manage the three of us, she said,
we will make it without fathers,
without grasping this half.
my mother not knowing her biological father,
but her daddy was James, and Luther
would never be my daddy just father,
we manage somehow in the quick stands,
the welfare lines, my mother studied how to live.
life, a little bit and gave us a chance to raise.

Native Rivers

there are satin flicks flowing from familiar ducts
like an ancient river rough native to the tongues of my soul
squatting behind the duckweed,
creeping slowly extracting the mistakes,
pulling dittos from minds, as a reminder of
my tempestuous youth, dubbing dreams,
hold, *once voided,* on stopped keys
i pushed play, now for keeps

there are native rivers dancing regalia sketched, drawn
in butterflies, hammered thin without breaking,
swinging capoeira agora crouched in position,
elevated in a puddle of three streams

praying to tributaries for the undulating movement,
pieced in time lapping its banks in idyllic pleasure
the country knows the sweet sweat tunneling out my ears,
hard hands helping the miseries form rage in peeled skin,
trees on backs, bodies hanging apples flooding branches
with their unwanted arrival

carrying on their torsos the stolen breath swaddled,
unsafe lost in the fracture of this lazy waterway,
gapped impatience pouring libation to hide,
the mixed nationalities, the resentment of this social sin,
pounce tempers flaring upward for creating me,
the abomination

Everybody Say Amen

our beauty shines
in the essence of our spines
raw bread splattered in butter
recalculating numbers
double jobs
'cause my children deserve the best

on sunday,
we ladies pray
for the sins of yesterday
we wash back existence and give gifts to Eve
our branches spring apples
'cause a praying woman holds-easy-families better

everybody say, Amen

see, we cup sensual breasts of current milk
honey spread bottoms, fire models desire spoken
in rainbow bridges, we touch policy papers,
talk real smooth and avoid the enviable

we are the dawn of morning's yawn
the shout of rays possessed on the beards of sons
and daughters, that spring our nations-creations

everybody say, Amen

say it tomorrow-*thank you*
breath life, re-cup butterflies
wish on ladybugs

accentuate the earrings
and strut yourself
for our ancestors--

Liberation

Closed flower girl in pink baby doll shoes
Bonding freedom quick sands of East wind
Barely fitting into a square of my own
Brawn future by pigtails, standing/fast
Muffled by a well-mannered youth
Zipped-tight under glass lids

Freedom was combed out ribbons
Hip-hugged jeans that cuffed my booty
And mama hated them, 'cos that meant
her baby was grown up no more spit licks
that equalized the ash on the rims of nose
or the Vaseline splattered all over cheeks
i would rather be cold

When I walked my feet would swish with air
kicked back on ankles cuffs undone that
made me look like a butterfly still arrived
in her cocoon wrapped in gauzed metaphors
bled judgment on the leaves, *do not return*

tummy was half empty still in need of nurture,
that licked breathe that only my mama could give, she
gave me back to Jesus, I hated her 'cos my love was not like
hers
Un-matured, cold from the streets of Homewood,
Eyes barbequed by the insults,
pushed

Kiss the lips and look at her
See the nights when she crumbled

on the tops of her bed in prayer,
grabbed her heart so, and I ran
fast

I felt her outline on the falling of the sky
she wanted to swaddle me,
her first daughter, once again

At Noon

at noon
lush rug cuts rolling mound
as dew of dawn gleams across pasture
is this utopia?
where land over flows
with milk and honey
whether march, may, or june
and the drowning seas of sky blue
hang clouds off rafters
until breathless noon
oh rolling fluorescent green hills
of bountiful glory
in which red and white man fight
for the love of land
where black man slaved hand over hand
for the love of land
and frontiersman travel with cover buggy
for the love of land

on sunday,
the only methodist white brick church rings
a clumsy swayed bell
and at noon,
women with long drawn out skirts
and extravagant hats
pillowing head as they lay
say their good days, so longs, and good byes
dedicated to the *"Almighty"*
they say
but we know, that they know

that inside the houses they pray
that God will heal the sins of today
and yesterday

across town
bronzed coffee-colored mills rust
remember yesteryear
when things were lucrative
but now it's a ghost town of
fluorescent green rolling hills
and smoked out pounds

with acid rain
and caddy shacks
that are laced with
embedded trees
that still breathe
aloud
soft sounds
now they must be closed and contained
and hushed for another time
by noon,
wake up Jericho
and tell the birds to come home
wake up Jericho
and tell the birds to come home

Maafa

75

let tongues
wither in shame
noose necks
exhaust
and breathe life
in bodies
that dangle
to execute
the demons
blood dripping
from Spanish galleons
they came in chains
swollen belly pregnant
with shackles
vehicles of death
lower deck
platforms
laying side by
poured in as
human cargo
hung ripe fruit
sweeter than
the days
grew long

the early
morning's chill
heavy fog
in between the
middle passage

demarcation of identity
creed lost in an instance
left on shores
footprints evaporate
with no trace
in the lands of beyond
the blotch that bears
a new name,
fixed right in their children's skin
worn, heavy-coated,
will never be removed
we are testaments
bearing witness
to the utter cries
the screams,
stranded off the ivory coast

Love Child
--for us

we lost our
baby somewhere
in-between the Kaufmann's
parking lot and our bedroom

i whisper to him, *later,*
i had a moment in darkness
like the one your having now
we cradled hugs and secrets,
with an obituary
to the moon

jeans bloody
x-ing the middle
of my passage
taken my love
away gently
lush fingers expressing
my empathy
lashing out sins
of the first born

taken to the heavens
cropped and snipped
tossed into succulent dust
new aroma from a
nine month dream
of a love child

once

there was a tummy
with elastic banded skin
pulling over a living being
growing into ten toes and torso
proud and smiling
a mama now,
a voided vision

Afternoon

mentally
physically
at a job,
swollen eyes look deeply in a mirror
at a wounded soul,
never was she a beauty but she had a job working
endless days
endless nights at--
got it right after college she did her job,
well, new boss,
new rules,
play by his books and
he'll be good to you
but she was never given a chance today
she lost her job, note on desk after meeting,
with reasons why she was incompetent
of handling her job,
fresh faces needed
to vitalize a company
that she helped create

work
day ends
going home
she lights a cigarette puffs twice,
then she throws it to the ground
she carried her spider plants home cardboard boxes
filled with eight years of work a picture

of her at the office, smiling tumbles to the ground
cars pass by
home
perspiration pours out of her body
how will she pay her car note,
how will she eat,
she runs bath water to the drain
bending over tears roll down,
her swollen eyes onto her cocoa brown cheeks,
razor sits under magazine,
deciding her fate~

Picasso's Angel

She could have been the model for
a water-colored painting,
porcelain blue-eyed wonder,
blonde curly strands,
that looked dollish with a red ribbon
so one day while playing,
on the yellow fire engine,
a five-year-old boy slightly bumped
her, pushing her off the side of a truck,
and the nanny ran to occupancy her,
holding her close

at first it was just a contusion
and after several tests-she still wasn't better
and after several tests it confirmed-**leukemia**
but no one had this history of—cancer
in the family

but she was going to fight it

five is supposed to be a big year of change
she was to have her Powder Puff birthday party,
with all of her girl friends in November
but today on the corner of Fifth and Meyran
she stood with her mommy
smiling after coming from Children's
three strands later,

of hair covering baldness
while her purple straw hat
they told her
she was in remission

Within These Walls

It was quiet when he came to her
Early in the morning he would kiss her
Tucking the satin sheets in
A frame sits on the corner of the nightstand
        Two people pose in a picture, *first date*
however, last night was not a symbol of love
        but a moment of devotion
when he told her that she wasn't pretty
to ugly to be with him
to fat to be his wife
never did she take heed
        she still loved him, *always loved him*
he always waited for moments when others weren't there
to be frantic and jealous
of her inner-beauty
something that he couldn't snatch from her
swollen eyes stare shut
within these walls
broken jaws,
fifty stitches going up
and a 3:30 call, *in the morning,* to the cops
the terrified women in apartment below
stayed in her comfortable cozy environment
while the screams and cries went on that night
while he emotionally wounded her,
pouring beer on her broken body,

their apartment
was like a sound proof box
families whispered

before her
around her
beneath her

angels all around her

sneering at her lies
her blacken-blue eyes lumped and bulging over her skull
and no one wanted to see what was so obvious
or what was so clear

she placed the blame on herself
once the proud ballerina
overcoming any obstacle
now so weak, *so frail*
barely holding up
how could a man do this to her,
                how could she let him
he lays beside her
cradling her bumps of, *"I'm Sorry"*

She could see beyond the coat of his foundation
His flowers and candy
                center-staged props
vanishing her vendettas
to be tortured forever in her mind~

Wonderland

my grandma taught me
the true meaning of sisterhood
when my auntie found
a mass in her breast
my grandma shaved off her hair
lush locks fell to the ground as an
offering for everyone who ever had cancer

i pant
while rubbing my breasts
in the shower
reading directions
on the plastic hook card

my grandmother gave me this as a present

i caress my daughters
worried about their future
i draw caricatures
that paint horrid pictures in thought
if i don't do it right,
if i miss the hardened pea
mistaking it for the average below my under arm

i think of aunts, who found lumps,
who weren't so lucky
thinking of pink bows

the soul beneath bone is terrified

i lug heavy scars
in my mind
taking an extra five minutes

looking in the mirror

lost hair follicles
toxin glowing in between my veins

I am too young for this
if I don't wrap my fingers and squeeze
        it will be too late for regret

eight years my family has walked on mother's day
all three generations
eight years for hope of a cure
power between them, will sort the fever
making sure that the fertility of this disease
dies in wonderland

Boneshaker

i had a conversation with america
told her to release ole souls still trapped in her green
told her to cut down branches that harbor canned fruit,

strange?

still dangling from its vines
-burn it as libation for my ancestors

i see lines about to explode
there goes promises and promises yet un-kept
unpaid labors for untold suffering
my skin is calling for blood, *scrapped*
my hair is calling for that 1865 field order
40 acres and a mule…

the survivors of Maafa
are under attack, *snatch back*
the 20,000 per person for Japanese-Americans got
snatch back the won reparations
and heal my people
we want education
we want healthcare
we want/we need

healing
we want communities restored
rehabilitation for our men

we want/we need

i am a boneshaker in search of satisfaction
female haley
this new bruise comes through
when ancestors keep calling
and flesh just didn't fuse the way white-hot tearing
had expected

this ignites then self-destructs like slow-burning coals
ready to implode a blaze

what is the body?

once it had groves
cells that make matter matter more
when your jail is your skin
and your skin is your home

shake-shake

i am running calling to the southern creole blood
in the plush of grounds-get up
it's time to restitute roots

the strictures of this narrative breaks skin
following this girl
reckless working days
quietly, don't forget me

and i can't
'cos their odyssey still lingers victim, flinching
defiant by gravity
chopped open

America hear your past...

it's calling bluesy like my spirit
i am restless for your answer

Women Come to the Front

scrambled legs

and run

from the

second wave

in the rubble

of twisted beam

bodies lie on top

and spirits rise

to see a new world

wives forced to

put on working boots

five cent in wage

while children's fingers

are used

as tools

grungy

and

dirty

after the war

is done

they all

will have a hand in it

not wanting to give it back

women grew power

got masculine over night

held offices to

kept cobwebs out

but after the chores are done

negro leagues

would play

shadow ball

bloodied

undefeated

baseball from the soul

Cedar Chest

the hooked metal hanger sat between feet, compressed,
stuck straight like the bobby pins in her hair
near the toilet, the crochet needle falling in the crack,
while she was bending over in pain,
it did not work the first time, *but second*
the blue towel that she sat in between her legs muted pain,
gasped for air, rimmed to blow on the tip of
her belly bottom, it tingled

when T, met V in a magic disappearing, act
snatching baby 3650, counting periods,
since she was eleven, flowing a way from the womb
she. Spoke, the river flowing encrypted in blood
ladled like dark chocolate gravy to her knees
it blew like smoke, complimenting the cedar
chest, stained, embossed in daises

the stale smell of spring sticky hot touching
reminding her of his flimsy dick pressed again
against her wall, back, in her little whore house,
on kitchen tables, she flew her underwear, *Lady Jezebel,*
let down her hair, and let the hyenas smooch
their lips in between yours, and whisper, on the oars of tongues

she remembers this all, splitting seconds, kissing her mouth ate
dress, she did the ritual that was handed to her, binding her from
her freedom-the paper dolls watched, her wrap in the breath
of her baby, throwing him in the incinerator, *tah-tah…*
she walks swaddled in her navy sweater, in the comforts of
home, tasting her choice, she can now can enroll in college~

The Gait Fought Stones in Serenade

i stare at sisters that have fought to exist in arms of evolution
just so they can see herstory in classifieds

the hollow of tombs riding on hinged gates to cancel back allies
examining obsessions of themselves, as second-class citizens

at the fingertips of husbands, no voice, cleaning pots,
triple load with babies, the flash backward tangled thorns

of a well mannered youth, living elegiac slurs caught in the lines
between the mattress, the silver lining-*their right to choose*

re-furbished, blank eyes, crossed, licking lips
to the sun crumbs, pacing, pacifist to abide their husbands

in ceremonies, voided, stripping, cargo, being girl,
holding tongues, missing womanhood into teddies

tucking tummy in at night, for the perfect hourglass,
she, like the dint of ideal wings, frigid gowns sliver to her knees

she seeks therapy for her soul, unlocking lipped passion,
in restraint for a thousand years

goddess, the golden lining--
her right to choose this life

Don't Forget the Fallen

Ties that bind her to the ceiling of the slave ship
So heavy are the shackles embedded in her wrist,
the sounds of chains ring like dusty liberty bells,
the piercing moans interrupting the calming
of her conscience as the vessel leaves traces
of ivory diamonds on the ocean floor.

She tried to recall the moment
she let go of her mother's hand
Her abba's promise to die for her,
But there was nothing she could do

She was forcibly removed from her family
Told to wipe their black from her porcelain face,
They made her sick with hopes
to find a cure a thousand leagues below the sea

They dragged her by the back of the neck and threw her in
warning her to be a good gal, the overseers'
pulled the cowry shells off her neck, your name is
"Ann," and she repeated her true name in Swahili,
The one that her abba pronounced under the quarter moon

The one that they rebuked and butchered with
their broken English tongue
Only to go retire to kiss their false gold
to toy with their babes in Toyland
playing with their tiki dolls after hours,
how was she was to return home

Already broken in, who would want her now
Unpure, unclean
when they stop for whisky at the slave trade
will she get her sweetness back
The poison out that they injected in her

There white semen, their white demon
Perhaps she should have been pushed over board
Before they railroaded her body
what lies under the vessel should not be feared
but welcomed release unto her spirit

Was she to go to her abba to put her head in his hands
And deny that she has been spoiled
But she wouldn't, she would be quiet
She would fill the breeze of her mother

She would hear the voices of the fallen
that sunk like a string of black pearls
to the bottomless hope
So she didn't cry out
instead she whispers don't forget
and the night wind echoes don't forget
The sea will tell

Off the Rocking Chair

Nestled in her misfortunes
her words became slurred
she just couldn't get give up the bottle
her dyed black hair became white over night
the quick sand embrace her ankles.

The person that *giveth life, taketh her own*
slowly into a premature grave
Oh forlorn mother,
On a door step a four-sided box remains half-empty
With a letter sticking out of his receiving blanket

His mother wanted him gone,
before he could be thrashed on a daily basis,
just like her already twice removed
Her arched head full of sadness
of no longer being mama,
No! not anymore
but she must do what's right for him and walk away
perhaps in the future she can search milk cartons
father scolded baby with hot water still relics

Like a rag doll shaken by loveless fingers,
time out was him being thrown in the corner,
held in a prison of tough love,
tainted love bestowed on a only child
he could have been the president of United States
the name carrier that real fathers need
now he will be added among the
collection of many hurt by family ties.

Beyond a Shadow of Doubt

Every Friday at 10:00 p.m.,
she would watch Law and Order: *Special Victims Unit*
looking for her story to appear,
searching for his face to show up on Most Wanted

Scanning through the mug shots,
recalling significant marks,
scrubbing vigorously,
the memory of him,
now, it's hard to wash down below,
where he left his scent,
his stain after they collected the evidence
scrapping follicles off the rug of her carpet
her chastity now under locked key

it took one year to find him after a traffic violation
a mere incident in Texas where they hauled his
gritty nasty self back to her,
secure the city, ***again***
hiding him in the cell

25 miles away from her safe comfy little loft
after two years of going through the same information,
recording the testimonies,
do you mind repeating that into the mike
the probing of her mind, not his
he gets away with 5-10 years?

the self-help groups she attended opened her soul, just a little,
recalling when she laid in the corner cupping her crouch,
swearing to take the long way home from now on,
attending secret therapeutic sessions
phone calls, *do you want me to stay with you tonight?*

could he have had the legal injection same as her

she was under oath
he was under suspicion

while the chorus lines murmured in chambers
no justice, no silence whispering to his lawyer,
"5-10 years, I want a retrial" the thought of him
getting a chance to appeal crossed her mind

so she eased out the door, undetected avoiding
eye contact with him while the NYPD scuffled
putting her hands over her eyes, she whispered, *No Comment*

they shouted, she gathering all the strength
to say again, *No Comment*
running down the stairs falling,
suddenly she falls out her shoe
her shoes are not made of glass and she isn't *Cinderella~*

Forgotten Places

Forgotten places like Black Wall Street,
Just to name a few, Rosewood, Wylie Ave
Became famous in their time.

Across the railroads stood a touch of blackness…
what could have been, what should have been
the rising of the Black Nation,
black towns, now deserted,
sad songs still blowin' the wind

Nightmares, flames, a bomb from the air
brunt to the ground by mobs of envious white faces
in ruins, a dream, lost chronicles…city records,
heritage yes heritage, was built with the little hopes of the people

Scant dozen of shamed-face houses scattered
Murdered, slaughtered, spirits coma' knockin'
at the golden door, that once held this beautiful creation
but helplessly it withered a way into a no/nothing town

Ghostly bodies from the 'Glades
where Ole' man Willie still hangin' to this day
so many nights, sounds have cried
people once, now twice
taken away from their homes

Bringing them back to slavery, helpless…
imaging the ocean breeze even the damp wood
that crept under their ancestors' feet, a hundred
years nothing has changed although everything
is rearranged

Their conscience feels the drums calling,
calling for a tribal meeting,
yet they run, yet they hide
disturbed images come to mind
seeing titled heads, their eyes watching God

Downtown Blues

A touch of gold is no longer in
the atmosphere for it has gone
Yet the dirt embedded urban streets still remains
The old jailhouse is still there

Even the railroad tracks along the river
Protesters still bother to come,
With signs for hope of a better future
The downtown blues sing a song
Of dreary harmonies
Of the good ol' days

Where men in their finest suits came across town
I'm just talkin' about the good ol' days
When everybody smiled
and the great depression was from town to town

Boys in their suspenders playin' tee ball
Little girls clutchin' their rag dolls
Their favorite babies… just to go shopping

The Blues

He done seen a lot, *I say*
He done seen a lot
Mr. Jazzman plays the blues
His potbelly flowing over his slacks
He done seen a lot

On his face five wrinkles,
his mama was a Baptist schoolteacher
She taught stories about slavery
So men in stiff white collars came with papers
She was thrown out of the classroom
for teaching Black Unity

No money for his family, he picked up his sax
And played on the street corners
For money to feed his six brothers and sisters,
In a one room house pots collect water
His mama died young,
Headlines read, "*Mother, found dead revolver to her head*"

His best friend Joe was found hanging
from a maple tree in just his drawers
He was twenty-three at the time
Death slapped a mask over his face
His eyes to the side
His tongue stuck out
Strange fruit on the tree
The rope burns were embedded in his sugar brown skin
His feet parallel to the ground
Yellow spot in front of his drawers

They tortured him,
He had just came back from the war
proud to have served his country,
He came decorated,
"*uppity*" they said
"*nigger*" they said
keep him in his place
strange fruit in a tree
hanging

he played the blues
on nights-open
he stood up and blew his sax
and moaned in remembrance
of the tender touch of stand still times,
they left tiny prints like autumn leaves
scattered across his body

the blues poured out
from deep within his pipes
as he blew to release his soul
which had been so cold
he howled at the moon,
wanting freedom again.

He done seen a lot, *I say*
He done seen a lot
His cheeks fall off bone now
From his lines of worry
God bless the child that got his own
That once had his own
His sax lets out a sour tune of
'Dem melancholy songs that play the blues~

Herstory

I will not find my liberation
by burning bras in demonstrations,
short-weighted, chained to a furnace,
asking you to respect,
the intimate songs through my soul,
walking through alleys,
for all those women lost by hangers,
cut and scarred in abuse,
plunged into coffins

So easy could I crumble in the wind
and forget that 'house wife' wasn't my first title,
ordained through the ovaries--
babymaker, can sometimes darken my spirits
long wind-stop-i ride,
my dynamic survival tempted
in dens with grenades
and even after i pasted the test

I stick out breast,
chin up and salute my womanhood
i-*blush*-and push through tears,
rumbled with my soul,
filtered from the warm movements of possibility
tickling in my womb--
weaved spanned at hips sited by the evolution
my swoop in spiritual-*supernatural, the sonrise,*
son who rose again, before the sunset
the stigmata that burns heavily in my soul,
and if only I could just touch his robe

then heal my identity,
this crisis-like a strand of beads
can't associate my womanhood with hysteria
my arms flap over my lap to
protect my goodies
the treaties of history

the roots are modified
through my steam
i slip through pipelines
hands full of grime
it doesn't dissolve easily
i forgot myself once--
headaches in stories
my divine sisterhood
needed struggle early on
so I would not have to do it
later

Free Ways

In center action,
these roving thoughts
in existing twists of eyelashes
they come sped slaved, like
Kemetic warriors on chariots
they expel in lingered stillness
that was once lost in the light
in the purgatory of burden flesh
I passed over by free ways, confined
In rough edges, tipped in sweeten ducts
I am reminded, that this butterfly
Is only a metamorphous shelled over
cocoon in old skin dropped in
promises' pregnant belly

They-are-still-here in me alienated
in the painted etches on pigmented pine-skins
loomed in bagged groceries
Put on the back-burner on idol walks on Penn Avenue
the stores I saw since 2
gone in tyrant hands
opened shop at 9:00 am
on North and Walnut
right in front of where my youth,
cornered sun-crumbs

I was taught to remove my poetry gloves
while severing smoothies with strawberries
on glass rims to cold stares
Can I take your picture?

grasp the memories
when I found my favorite blue pen
when the center of my world screamed poetry
the sweaty memories of metal fans
cooling only, the edge of my legs
my tears, frozen I found me
the musty smell couches
and dimmed lava lamps
traces of poetic tea made from scratch
I salute the memories well

Butterfly Beginnings

<u>Rites of Passage</u>
I enter a maze of confusion
Of a history that is so ancient
And I just can't run away
As the djembes beat heavily
my heritage is entwined within me
My grandmother's father's mother dreamed of a better life
Now through me
I can see it--
I embrace it--
I walk into it--
<u>Womanhood</u>?
Babe on hip I walk
And an aura has punctured
the youthfulness of my person
Into the direct tranquility of the waters--
Motherhood?
my mother
was mama
and daddy
nurtured me, integrated me
into an abstract form of life
and lead me through the fire
        of my internal
<u>Rites of Passage</u>
I learn that my womanhood didn't begin on
my 18th birthday
but in this lifetime--
now--

I promise that tomorrow is mine
I promise that tomorrow is mine

    enclosed in a box

     I console these adult feelings
I knock out the insecurities within my heart
And learn the difference between will/want
and on a scratchpad I write
I will declare my will
I will be self-reliant
    yet
I am drawn into
pleasure seeking wants and desires.

Fallen Bittersweet

a dream,
deferred
has been trampled and set aside
for the next generation to wonder
no one mends it
or tends to it
school bells ring year after year
as fallen leaves yawp
drifting to the ground
a reminder is conjured to former you

muses that once soar
breathing thoughts and rhymes
have been hushed
seizing the day is harder
fallen angels that soar above head
don't secure imaginings
lost youthfulness that has withered away
and the waste of talent
your compassion
is left to fertilize the lilies

Power of Sisters

While I was climbing oak tress looking in branches,
held up by standing demons
breathing intoxicating fumes,
in white tee shirts dancing to encrypted music,
bouncing rivers that roared in
ears flexing my mouth open,
I was resending cognitive messages,
reorganizing, decomposing my blessings
written in the stars

she will be the mother of nations

"In this house we praise the Lord," ma-ma said
realizing the gifts that God bestowed unto her, again
but there was child of God hidden-soft sweet-sister
eight years younger-came and claimed my spirit for me-
You know Jesus loves, you *right*-she said to me singing, started
worshiping in tongue force feeding my soul,
pouring holy-terrific-juice down my throat, tears swelled

My nine-year-old sister kissed tears,
washed my feet,
cloaking me in the blood of the lamb
smiling her heart of fire fierce--
"In this house we praise the Lord"
say it *Shae*-**say it now**-*Shae*

So I said it

claiming the mysteries foretold
the day I was born out of baked dirt,
chosen to be put in ma-ma's arms
the special one--

under the oak tree,
finally listening-*breathing*
i learned he had been waiting-sitting-
trying to visit me--
to rename me as his daughter
of warriors to come.

Out of the Ashes

her hair sits
like wild fire
bracing the lion's tongue
she perfumed the summer
fed the lake
with the
slow passing
of her arm
her apple cheeks squishy
lifting our spirits

waiting eight years
for her to grow
out of the ashes

from the moment
she perceived life
joined me in sisterhood
i wanted to help her
weave small wisdoms
through the fabric

kiss love bruises from her
smooth butterscotch skin
loving her from the world
because she is the beauty of the ashes
that sits unharmed, innocent

i want to teach her
what tomorrow holds

extracting
the scent of graveled pain

i hear her yelling her emerge
and I want to
suppress it
grind it
and throw it away

Trails of Lace

I am lost in shadows explaining why my tenses are black
We marched trails of lace with out logic
Bestowed in memories--
of dirty piled up heaps
Side-by-side,
my dress got stuck between
the hugs,
Patting me on my shoulder,
I am so sorry for your loss
I, the first granddaughter

The color wind dropping down mocha cheeks
I should have known you more
stared straight to your face
Remembered--
pressed you in my memory
What you looked like--
kissed you longer--
loved you harder

but for that brief second

GR and I stood holding each other
right in the left corner where the silver
handle rested on the grass
we share memories that no one
could ever touch

We hugged so tight that the air lost life
and feel in-between legs
We thought of childhood laughs,
like brother-sister so many years
Goodbye.

Goodbye just like old relationships closed doors

we remember the horse drawn carriages in Schenley Park
and we were amazed,

our family house brings memories
of our potato chip trains on plastic-cover
couches encircled by our aunts
smile for the camera

Today-*tonight* we have been walking
in others' dreams-nightmares
Asking questions
Hearing echoes of yesterdays cry

My cousin holds his Kleenex between his thumb
His legs spread, *I follow on his lap*
he left tears on my dress
the one i never wore again
the one i left hanging off hangers 'cos it too
remembers my pink blossom
the day i changed directions,

it is me. this young lady
swallowed in this sadden vortex lazy sweeping my spirit

breathing beneath dirty sheets and coming
out in the Grand River Yarns
unraveling

it is me, the sweet spirit dust touching
my grandfather's body
four years and he still spreads tears
monsoons my spirit
it dangles
holding me secure

When My Black Children Run—

When my Black children run to find
cover away from dismay
What will I say to them
When they tried to find their Black beauty
       within,
What will I say to them?
When they try to find respect, love, and dignity.
What will I say to them?
          mountain
      the
     over
I will say   you are Black
Across the water you are Black
         Up
   lift our hands
When we   we will call on a new world.
When we lift our hands to the everlasting skies
you won't have to run to find beauty
     within,
It will be secure and waiting,
Love runs deeper than blood and the blood runs
deeper than water.

Through the Woods

our baby butt cheeks slice into the bars of heaven
flirting with the braces
while licking dullness by the sacks of our souls

we *hold blue jackets*

hauling liberty on our spines
overused insanity brews anger tea while
we are quivering, dehydrated
looking at people in the window
of the nearest family restaurant
we watch them suck down chicken bones
sipping sprite with ice

we recollect our storm

trudging to our cardboard gingerbread house
soggy slippery from last night's monsoon
it now frames a picture for the sky

our hallow stomachs bare, shaken
in a stranger's hand
escapes the open
prayers of night flourished
now forgotten promises
that innocence absorbed
snapped pushed into
the gritty earth

pause

dry salads
glob of miracle whip

hungry anyone?

down the line
pushing shoving
for the last piece of fruit
our crushed stamped feet bare example
marked in hunger
2 mile hikes to the
nearest christian shelter
getting closer
across the train tracks
and through the woods

Like a Thousand Words

my soul is like a thousand words, *unspoken*
put away with rusty blankets
my dreams are like liquid silver flowing tight ropes,
clasped on tempt words that only sing songs around my neck

in the first eclipse,
on thursday
january 12, 1980
born

i was **born** to speak tongues anointed at my fingertips
rising above cold suns, love tomorrow, but
let it be sold, *sold*
like old souls kissed,
my spirit was once juicy fruit
smacked in jaws, *enjoyed.*

now, tunnel vision got me on
hard feet climbing uneven roads
the dusty splatter in my internal rites of passage
i am the opal of the ivory seas
sold passing gazing moons on vessels

redeemed precious metal belongings to the other
am i the lyrical daughter of eve?
am i lounging on my ancestors' lives?
like i lost the bite that wheeled the spirit
transformed skin to a smoother existence
black to queens and kings- *higher beings*
now sealed-open

channeling life to breathe into this ancient yawn
pouring libation from the hips of apple trees
i heave black on my back,
stools on mobs unable to see
my blue blood meeting oxygen
my heart bleeding,
flesh touched skin
bones gripping cavity-human
breathing-*life*

i could once strip the wings off butterflies
paste them to my armpits
shudder at their evolution
but rejoice, only existing when they are changing positions

feel me, cutting pods out their awakening
in imaginings they have become a
pot luck womb primed
under a whole new identity

i have seen me before jumping,
in side my self-pulling poison
dazed in sweet-sweat
hoping to catch my breath
wanting to drink out streams, almost relieved

becoming a cliché item,
buried in forked skin plush
woman scorned?
almost, i can just taste the better line of life/deaf
clapping, welcoming home
dancing in acclaimed democracy

A Tribute to Loving You

I was warned
how to love,
you

tripping over booby traps
to your liking
hugging your spirit
to calm you down
rubbing knees
warmed milk
to show you
i was not the disappointed one
that left you brokenhearted
misshaped,
motionless,
with no warning

you don't have to scrap
for food in canisters
to escape in the open
angry at breath
catching existence
for me to hold you near
to want you, **bad**

unconditioned
relentless, beauty you are
i wonder what you could have been
given a chance to break
the covering from your unsteady legs
later in life

your words
drying out the cactus flowers
that holds you in bondage.

*Catch22

hair tied back away from my face
limping through lines-*I press shirts, now-for a living*
the memory when we were runaways

under the bridges of Shenago County
when we ate skins of orange zest to satisfy our tummies
licking dried beef stew off cans to savor the taste in our
throats—

falling through the cracks
under shingles and snuggled wishes

it was catch 22 falling down on my knees
that made us move back home again

looking in want ads over Mama's house
eating Captain Crunch on her couch

Iron City Uniforms
Of hard pushes my soul
Now work...

the smell of sweat swearing angry at my skin for pouring out
holding down handles, steam press, hang steam, press
hang, hold shift feet left rub again.

Again-stolen notebook pages ripped reading between
flipping and studying on turned backs
pushing pieces of smashed toilet paper in shoes.

"these work boots hurt me feet" I whisper

stripped bare shaved down to the core,
stuffing shoe soles digging in between my toes.

the maker's did not intend for us to see the installation
the lath where I can finger holes nestled down deep
my swollen ankles slipping.

down in the gut where the logged nail embraces
plowing through my virgin skin clattering down on pain
the back, scratching tendons rubbed red.

"what a hard life," I whisper to my neighbor.

Demonstrating the Art of Love

when this morning
abruptly appeared
my hand wipes
the other side
of our bed
your silhouette shadows
and you weren't there
this morning,
"told on you!"

the gloomy sun shines down
on me
as i sat
in the corner
waiting for a phone call
to hear your drunken voice
list excuses of bewilderment with nonchalance tones

putting on my knee-high nylon boots
cold
white covered blankets
on the ground
i slush feeling my boots absorbed, *heavy*
hurting and torturing my spirit
the omen of your soul
whispered gently in my ear

where could you be,

this morning
buttons
fumbled on
my winter coat sloppy sided

i didn't care…

i pulled down the yellow hanky
barely covering my head
with the Steeler print
particularly, showing the brown mess of hair

i kept walking
braking into the
freshly coated snow
pulling your prom picture out
looking
very slowly,
as tears streamed out my eyes
my hands like window wipers
pulling away
seeing
when you looked like a little man
half grown
smiling
at your best
in case you were on a milk carton

slurring my words,
tripping over my own feet
walking to the police station
i reported you
missing

Chair

the day that granddad died
i squeezed the pimples from my face
unplugged the phone
knuckle punches ready to win the war, *for him*
i slept in between two winds
veil covered, his memory served me
the taste of mild Old Spice
and musty work clothes left on the hook
awaiting for his healthy arrival
but this house, hold, would not see him again

he must have known that it was time to go,
when the door chimed, *"Joy to the World,"*
and Ma-ma heard the message clear,
us grieving, savoring his smell,
his brushes full of his salt-and-pepper hair
said he was gliding heavens,
he visiting us in our dreams and all,
that's why it felt so incorrect going
back to see his things placed
I should have called him, more in my regrets
We cried, holding our family closer this time,
missing one person my aunt whispers,
"God takes the strong for his army" we smile
we kissed angels at his memorial and
saw granddad for the first time since Thanksgiving,
his hands heavy hard preformed, placed
cupped over his heart admired brown catty
piece in place, meaning peace, meaning
 soup often thought to have a home

a postmark
the way i collapsed in fathoms past the pulse

the thickly coded paint
made him two shades darker
pushing his cheeks off bone
his suit did not fit his spirit, I thought
this color was not him, I thought
and so his soul moves on…
clothed to face heaven not belonging to a church
opening mouth words grew backbone
heavy eyes stumbled to cry pushed out
tired, walking up stairs
i fell asleep in my grandfather's chair

Stall-A Wife in Waiting

I stall out-another tough night, pleading
Hiding my $10 stash, the only thing left after
You saturate yourself in liquor
The move where points wait
And I am nailed down too long to be quiet.

Hush-remember he is not in his mind
the empty feelings are just like hiccups
ring-*it not you*-home is distant from your memory
your feet smell of dirty dots of inconsistency
and I wonder if I am trapped in prints with no directions

no exit arrows or bedtime rubs, lavish gallons of water
drink it down Shae-for your sugar
you knew my remedy before I could speak
just dropped kisses of goodbyes
no time to ask me how my day was,
or did I take my medicine

I am use to being the selfish one
jumping on floated breath,
bowed to your every command
don't tell a soul-*you say...*

Sigh...

The only time I can feel your spirit is
When you sober mind transfers into its lovely hood
Becomes *soft-spoken-no-longer-existing-***RAGE**
From your 23-year-old hibernation and I know

You hunger is looking for redemption, your mind
Rolls on my lap…

and I don't know who is sick
me for being in love with you
or the thought that maybe you will change.

I-dentity

half my i-dentity slipped through the fingers
of my grandfather in to the back woods
of North Carolina's cold mountains
never connected its self to father
so i am fumbled fingered with numbness
barely able to grip this newfound history
this cradle of evolution, has demented seed
that i reckon

trying to rotate its place into some characterization

my reality and fiction is mixed,
'cos all i remember is Mama
her struggles and father looks like me,
but trans-parent
i hug my soul for staying close to home,
to the streets of Pittsburgh

i i-mprint my spirit
before the washing of the brain, occurs
i belong, somewhere else
my culture determined its self-long, before.
almost prehistoric, when God willed me life
i was molded like the likeness of him

i am gonna send a hologram
that i am full off my other side
so it will send a telegram to
break branches from the oak tree,
sow them to the torso of time
its pending greatness, *i taste its nectar*

flowing like hot lava ready to explode

my i-dentity cannot be defined
in the form of fleshy cells
cast over in battle dressings,
counting pulses soaked in biscuits
only tipping scales to birth

my i-dentity is pulsating scripts on waterfalls
dripping into my aura, one tear at moment
latching on tilted wampum
slow on djembes down thighs,
in the foot-prints of, **I**.

Sing Against My Silence

there are hushed pauses in my life
think back, rewind
received flashbacks on how it was to smile
i lay in salvia's sweat swearing
shaking time to listen
throwing spears into my belly button
close to death

turn back the pricks
the five wounds on rotated thumbs
spilled-dropped in dots-that slave my life
slip through fumbled fingers
while dark moves through shadows
bearing its claws against the sun
these hands-*tangible parts*
i should be taking small sips
absorbing the hemoglobin
inspection-statistic-snapshot

i will sing against my silence
my mind is stretched-worn folded
back in the closet of when i was a little girl
a new dress was mama's remedy
my body slumbers when it wants
back in years when worries censored

administrating finger sticks prematurely,
living at random, the cold shakes,
massages, thoughts of later in life
so i am classified in this rite.

Reclaiming Items in My Closet

sometimes, when i open my closet,
pushing hefty bags off the tops of shoeboxes,
pulling hangers from dresses to pants,
looking at boxed up poetry-*crammed tightly,*
scared to lose a phrase

where bitten pencils are behind long amish dresses
that hide knees-*just for church*-to rid the sin-
the plus size clothes premature--
dark to hide my shame of pale shades-*of me-*
dying the sky as evening shatters the afternoon

in color scarves hunted in armpits,
looped around my tongue,
swallowed by the essence of
wanting to feel young again
i am dreaming of muted beaches
sand gook on old nike flip-flops
running across melted dunes

i want to love myself,
i have the right not to remain silent,
get a whiff of chaos-*even* tripping-
where future resembles past-*alive*

i know my complaint--
and you can't rape me anymore
you can't spit in my face and ask me for a rain check
you can't take my hopes away from me

you can't enslave me--
put back the shackles, now
--separating the sound

i will be slipping markers for refuge--
stopping wind with one finger-*now*-
i am reclaiming items--
plugging corners with rat traps.

The Colors of My Love

I have been a believer of Nubian gods
Promising me that they will
Give me the world with a twist
Of a finger-my soul weighs a
thousand pounds of madness-
Walking--believing that they could
Give me what I lost in between the war
Balance the sun when the atmosphere
Isn't paying attention

I have nodded my head after
My lips were taped shut, in the guff
of my throat, I choked on believing
in their secrets still extending my hand
at their welcoming table, yielding to their
demand I became braless

My whipping wasn't by lynchers
But on top of bedspreads
Holding headboards, later asking
them to love my spirit
they bleed refuge through sutures
the empty feelings, where the
colors on my palette became diluted
with one touch of a brush

I pushed back my tattered remains
Trying to erase time-exhausted,
Later it came back with a vengeance, it bathed
In a orchestra of democratic voices,

it pulled me up by the sleeves, telling me to wake up,
while shaking sleeping babies and holding them to death,
It blew its way right to my face, and fought for
Me to comprehend-used
But, I am not bitter…
The colors of my love have mended songs
that flow through out my flesh
It has categorized *father*-as being my
First failed relationship, it has given me dittos
of late night phone calls I begged for someone to love me
my middle showed gravity empty from the rejects
of never receiving a gift, they wanted my kiss
but never wanted my soul.

Less

I am less without home,
a triangular space where my couch
empties out nightly, a bed and dust
the mist of air tasting like
stale breath un-neutered

my possessions in a semicolon-space-waiting
for its next journey, it wants to spill out of
its corners needing Ritalin; showing me
the secrets of spinning back fist, yelling
for everyone to move out its way.

I am a slave to cold chills
streets and bums are just one notch under me
my shopping carts are filled with 5 years of life
tastes of remembrance when things weren't so complicated

there bars on my back have tattooed themselves
all over my body pinching dollars to wake up
this metamorphous is stagnant crying for simplification
but time is a fatty piece of breast that will not lactate

so I wait.

Scattering the Ashes

in this house we exist in memories
        pictures before my time
        and stories that we re-birthed
        my new cousins will never
        feel the warmth this home has held
        Its quiet, oxidized, out of practice
        foliage has lost leaves, and
        big wheel competitions,
        family singing while granddad is watching
        football with the boys.
        they pass their stories with wild parties
        remember when Joan ran away
us kids smile and could probably
        repeat the same stories just like our parents
        for our own young, *it never fails*
        we never want those stories lost
        our heritage so pronounced at an early age
        my cousins like brothers and sister
        extended we are the ashes that rose from the ground
        we scatter the visions, what is left of us by word of mouth
        at thanksgiving, my aunties passed the dollar
we are now adults we must bring one dish
        and pray in a circle about what God has blessed us with
        GR says something, we pause look up, laugh
        we turn our attention to Kevin and Karl
        for going to college, nana stands for
        those who are missing, Jimmy and Joan
        granddad's spirit in the middle of the circle
we are better than Soul Food, our series will never end

Carolina Hills

almost like,
i was adopted seeing my family
for the first time

the nervousness, came--
of a memory, pocket green-binded
Bible highlighted with passages
re-introduced its self.

everything about me
had been roasting in the Carolina hills
i-became the eight year old back in time,
smells of greens and hog maws echo...they call

mimic my youth,

ready to confront curdled feelings
all alone

off the bus, i dropped my luggage
kissed my father on his cheek
our i-dentical moles matched,
my key..let-ting open

it's one step closer, this time i didn't run to him
like how characters do on television
lift my left leg up in arched L,
happy to see Luther and embrace him
--*just a simple hi-* our new adult relationship

i am finding where i fit in,
the reason why i came, **here**

that type of high,
on cloud 48/23--25 years in-between
insecure, my father doesn't know me

i study him, stare at his eyebrows
paint them with my finger on face-*they match*
where do i belong?
--today,
i forgot about the disappoints,
my father missed why?

i became daddy's little girl, *in one instant*
my synopsis was ready to dump every
idea i ever had, just-to-feel my imagination
get a whiff of being whole.

Beyond the River

He wants me to forget that I am human
mend back the pieces of my heart
re-dig up my rings at the bottom of my
purse and just push past--

My emotions are etching their own direction
they exist even if I swallow a thousand pills
just to wish away my dreams.
HE IS KILLING MY SPIRIT

I am a runaway trying to redefine my extensions
and to calculate my pockets. *I am less without a home,*
in an attic above the newly painted house my mom built
crammed words gravitate on canvasses
blank empty screens staring back me

2 weeks he hasn't called and a little girl
was just found in back of the stadium down
the street in Wilkinsburg.

I want to see that face

that means somewhere he is living
across the bridge...beyond the river

i could almost taste his breath
his realization that he stayed too long away from home
this time I didn't call the police,
he will find his way home when the pattern
eats at his soul and deception has cultivated
in his obtuse version of life.

This Life-Cipher

I fell in love with a married man.
My sobbing feelings are manipulated
into a clay model platter exempt from
ever being his one true love.

We never thought our partners would fight
so hard for us. There are invisible feelings
knotted in caressed thought as his seed
grew into an apple beneath my navel
linking us three together.

No longer does he want to be sequestered.
Only after the baby is born, I wear my Scarlet
A in my belly growing, *Alone*. I am caught
within the scaffold of his diseased heart.
His lips cushioning love songs
played backward on self-afflicted
hate notes.

I evoke the recipe captured in my womb
Small bites, in between our showers,
in remembrance of my former self, I pour out
my obsession, I want him for keeps, the beggar
in me more selfish then ever on the nights
he claimed she was nothing more than a legal--
wife typed on paper, he told me his
feelings were growing more intensely for me.

This life-cipher holds a 360-degree spin
one with upheavals thoughts looming
have pamper requests. I'm pleading and
he won't answer that call either.

Desert Saints

i am dreaming of rainbows ripped in reverse
when promises bleed through sutures

desert saints,
left on the outskirts at the end of the world
grace is folded in the clouds
amen,
is forgotten.

isolated churches,
sheets of webs climbing
revisiting gomorrah
defiant by the quotes of revelation
amen,
is forgotten.

scriptures ripped in crusades
evil inquisitions quote marks of the beast
there are dark spaces

gapped

that bare heavy hearted fists beating
bible school showdowns in evolution lynching lies.
those, turned away empty pocket
screaming at God why they are left in the dust,
but no calls the unwanted
the rapture that lifts the spirits
grabbed ghost faced shouting to the ground

"TRUMPETS BLOW YOUR HORN"

pushing world war three under key
the wrath of salvation that clothes the question
protecting, paneled in purple and gold
a personal savior,

on bended knee when irrefutable proof
is on the scale of faith life hangs in
the balance
prophecies are cheering for the heavens
amen,
is remembered.

Canvas
-for Dre

his mellow lyrics demand a presence
he rocks my soul
i will see him when the sun shines red
pluck chords, rhyming hooks
letting melodies flow of his fingertips
his rhymes tenderize my soul
he taps me on fire

spiritually to interludes on toned hums
it is his awareness that holds me in contempt
or the moment we made something beautiful,
i struggle for words
that i love--*more than i should*

his efforts, fork my dreams into tranquility
fleshy, *raise of libido,*
pulsing on the lines of jeans held tight
it is his speech that moved me
i walk only at the of rims of his poetic mind…
speaking with my days of soft thought clashing

how can i define my need to feed,
on his words, a thirst to get drunk off his thoughts,
a means to invade his dreams
i wonder if i can spread bridges on canvas just to touch
the ambience of his spirit.
he is a single strand of ancient honey
slurping joy of his bronzed skin

Dream-Girl

I almost drowned myself
in a dream

the reefs took me by the fatty-part of my arm
and lead me into the abyss
there were lights that illuminated
echoes and negatives of human figures

What is underneath
            sometimes rises to the surface.
They say that in heavy rains
the balance of mass-water
floated to air
i raised my palms slowly
slightly to shout save-life

I would have rather stayed nestled in my mother's womb
then to find that I no longer have a place, I exist
in the out box, be the free child that has no boundaries
if i would have known in latter years
that it would be this hard to breathe-*eat*

i would have slipped into the abyss
with no cares

see earth from a distance
as an angelic being,
this world would then be christened with my kiss
gigantic from this memory

Song of a Sister

i am channeling the hurt that beckons empty hours
an improbable journey winging the mist of laden mountains
above the redwoods arched over burden
somebody is breathing in me sun kiss from the neighboring
continents where their skin knows me by name

i am in the same room with the beast of revelation identified,
promising he will take my imperfections
in the sizzle of ember pushed against cool soft skin
this song of a sister surrounded by halos with thorns of
deception.

nestling dormant in the base of my spine
into the sweet golden mango meat
i pray

i am more native than yesterday,
held the blackness of my soul offering the dirt to my smile
unveiling the darkness in the quiet of the eve sneaking into my
spirit

this song of a sister,
i weave constellations of intoxicated lullabies
to sweetly soothe my will to weep,

i am a big girl now whispering hymns of devastation
i cry mending holes in my socks
sliding down rails
i do not think about the impossible

the hundred stories about maintaining balance
i now find dialogue among the writers
hat's off servant girl
conformed to illusion

What I Could Not Tell You

I was dropped in mid-journey too afraid to open my mouth--
clawing out my swaddled breath and empty thoughts, belly down
subsiding out green ankles docked hate without saying
descending from the years of your not good enough to be--
the hint of shyness examining at dinner tables
sudden stumbles slipping in parched shade at bowed commands

(not being comfortable in my own flesh)

This was a learn change caused by fumbled feelings
pressed in sorrow-of seasons distorted
tapered on the side of my forehead
i remember the day the noise fell into my lap
the night that the river drunk cups of tea
dressing in dark blue scars no longer matching my color

(i am a coward)

Leaving in waiting caught in revamps
there is a feeling my heart
in the bends of hands caressed in spirit
i have fashioned on tattered napkins
burden by the exterior

Burning inside of me, revolution noose knotted
compelled to show the world my sorrow
to exist in the whirlwinds of kissing times
opening lips parched on sedative rims of beer bottles
in the quick sands suspended in motion

Exploration of being in the twist of washed hands
there is guilt in goodbye
the yoke of sadness in lucid dreams-deferred
hard hitting beast visiting memories in gallant breezes
what i could not tell you was that my happiness
failed on deaf ears too consumed to understand
the body in my inner thighs

Slicing my soul thin spread
delicate from the hand's of butchers
closed down by truths echoing tears
i stand near buried by the piled up demons
shoveling prayers, *excuse me sir*
lifting my scars raised in crusades
declaration is standing

On the Road Again

i pack up the corners of my segregated life
that won't fit in a box
never forgetting the cement floor that was once my pillow
or the begging of Christian shelters
when my stomach was empty and bare
wild
crazed
girl
once
ungrateful

Daunting thoughts of adulthood
Raced speed boats in mind
Never in my wildest dreams did I think
I would be
running
from bad landlords that have abused my youthfulness

i am a runaway
never existing
never understanding what it is to live without fear
never did get a chance to be rambunctious
having pockets of money sag my pants
or the chance to go on a formal date

courting

I met my match
starting our new unplanned life
leaving Mellon

putting peach-colored walls in the back of our minds
i just can't wait to be on the road again
in a new apartment

the best given in Pittsburgh
secured by faith
not by love
this will be home, i will say one last time
as i tape the top with all the memories of former year
throwing away the pain i caused
but i will not stay stuck in this warp-hole
of time
i smile
kissing my husband
not scared to face it all.

Stench

your shoelaces left marks in my carpet, *again*
i scrub my rug in bleach yet your essence remains,
marked-*here*

here to days that display long regrets in bags packed,
we should have listened to our families,
but we were too busy climbing fences
sneaking in our friends basements,
and fucking…

you took my virginity away
kissed both the hot line of chocolate hands
reclaiming marshmallow dinners--*don't eat it all*
remember Schenley Park, when we tripped on beer cans,
and wondered if we could swim or get swallowed in the gulf?
i put your hand on my belly and so--
We will be in love forever--
Amen

the procession of my spirit
too young to know our demons would ride on Hey-rides
you forgot what love was, so innocent-*daring*
Slipknots between our tongues
taunt these days to ever step between us…
i don't know who we are
where be, but the truth is I did a lot alone
and sometimes the moon cries,
at nights, in our bed i roll seeking your presence
but only your stench remains

Tarnished

the song upon your thick lips, your grace
the seething iron with your flesh
your mangled reflections to shadow
the spell of stillness, a promise to
never shatter the same cold hand
that is not stumbled upon confession,
only committed to the whispered prayer
to memory, my fingertips, land flamed
butterflies from the orange blossoms come
down to the irises and take a sip, *i am called freedom*

where wine glasses come in a jar, inside life tokens
carried on a string *here*, green jewel bottles capture
the romance lasting through a kiss
i am the stopper of the sunshine filtering
through the abyss golden dragon's wings
hanging in the azure, misted elves and daisies
join together in the laughter where iridescent
bubbles join between the you and i blowing magic
faerie dust from opened hands

particles lie hanging in the air circled eyes
are encased in feathers from the clear,
cold air of an upper atmosphere storms
affect the limits are in our imagination,
a quiet place secret and solemn hidden by
the raging waves of the sea shaded by willows
and fragranced by lilies the bright sun shining
down on us rolling hills bright green and fresh
where fields of roses lay i ask for entirety

but it is now too late, to propose idol
dreams, now tarnished every footstep that
tiptoes close behind your silhouette a demand
of ceaseless hum touching upon my skin.
my small hands were not so easy to grasp for you
that they forbid your timely escape in fragments
safe for your eyes to seize my being

two halves of one breathtaking whole my
restless nights, I miss you diminished in spins
twisted in harmonies reverence unrequited
so I am asking you to walk away do not
haunt my spirit again

Learning How to Lay

we play tickle insomniac
until the wee hours of the night
stargazing neon constellations
tucked between the arms
pinned under covers
the new uneasy feeling of security
trading bunk beds for
the snoring howls of his roaming voice

he is the found victim
of my single sleep wild untamed

after the first year

we felt comfortable in different corners
got attached to each other's cutlets
beside intimate under trade for held hands
and rubbing sweet faces
detained in crevices

i see us like characters in movies

uncomfortable, lasting after sex, reality
our toes touch a sign that our love still glows

now the third year

i slightly lay tilted
under him, evolved under his shadow

i submit to his sloppy handling of my body
he slips arms over my curvature
sneaking peeks of my breast
in between fast turns
how cunning gentle beauty
into a slumber, i am
use to his feeling
practiced

Too Close to Home

there are fewer men tonight,
that cannot find their way
the dirty streets that they walk on
have paved their way

i am more indulgent to their cries
i know they are not nameless
that the parked bench is their friend
and the moon is their streetlight
mouths empty, huddled, stomach
families

[their story is worse than mine]

these faceless men creep under dark shadows
these faceless women under bridges that hustle
scrapped throwaways,
crawling on the T, sharing sidewalks
while pleading for cups of coffee

i see their reflections in my eyes
i squirm because my appetite has grown
forgetful not remembering
i once had a notion
now middle class,
i sing it from veins
i spin my own history, in retch,
in dreaming
of bed sheets
in luxurious security,
i dream it

i scare easily holding my purse, **tight**
dashing across the streets
the smell is there
the voices of the underground echo nightmares
of repeating my three-year-old story again
the men who stand on elevated boxes in the marketplace
shouting
for pennies
are too close to home

Our House Is Numb

Before words cocked showdowns
fury flagged space in between our hearts

I watched us struggle in cupped places
In the hollow of throats hard-bitten

Hours of anger dwindled to shallow breathing
Half asleep on the couch
We pay restitution for robbing our home of comfy dreams
bloomed spirits that brought the world between us
playing catch up, **now**

Passing memories around the dinner table
washing dirty hands in the basin
Tangled in vines nothing, but
a cigarette tossed into a bowl of silver smut
remains

no words with sturdy looks
up-and-down
I pack my book bag
I call my best friend
Do you have any room?

And my Christian-2 minutes outdoor attitude
wants to run away
From the three years I fought for us to exist

Being the back bone, the rock of us
But then the door looks further away from my feet
His face stamps heavy head on my mind
And I can't move

Redden Eclipse

In my youth the stare of new words,
rushed lips, the ending happened quite suddenly
remember my mama's steps
we made love on the kitchen floor
two inches from the dinner table
exchanged words 6 months
while walking miles to Wal-Mart
kickstand love courting
only four years later

i panic reading those words again,
our music holds fresh roses in a CVS bag,
steady notes from the city...
we puffed on the 6th St Bridge
right under Clemente's bat

(we)
surround-sound steel valley,
redden eclipse had an
argument-in the slits of fog

we are like the highways
you skate through my body like the ice-capades
bright lights reminding me of moon lights
when i held you in my arms for the first time
paced- tranquility grabbed the whites of our eyes
uncovering our future

I caught a glimpse of alphabetic silence-
empty handed/taste of hard breath floors from- push

dedicated to invisible dances halfway to the scaffold
amber bruises barely shown fear from harped anger lashing
too quick for me to dance a way
I saw silence explode out torched late night stains
Yawns creeping across backs ached in spirit
My "**V**" cushioned by boxed in arms
Cover face, look over uncoiled

Loud mouth-zipped
our four years like centuries

we stared at empty bellies while
eating skin off chap lips
barely room to surface our scared tomorrows
our lavish meals once a month
testimony to the tales
i fought like hell
to separate bars and beer
from our marriage

our four years like centuries

on front tails
when all we had was each other
we gave everything to God
clouds dropped pieces of bread for us
miles before this bridge ever came

You Can't Control the Wind

silly girl,
you can't control the wind

or the blood
it haunts you like thick smells of momma's soup
the first time nigger even came into your dimension
and showed up so close
that it scorched-flesh-deep

silly girl,
you can't control the wind

or the after effects and shocks
that points, ignorantly on cold nights
or shouted words, taunted bluff

silly girl,
you can't control the wind

or hair on late mondays when you read
relaxer boxes creamed up your scalp, "perm,"
your hair like momma did since you was five years old
'cos her momma put that conk and only diluted down for you

the long laces of creole roots keep tunneling
keep reaping, keep bouncing off your wound
still fresh from that monday's perm when
you tried to comb out that "nègre" and brush it away

the rich history that rummages in your blood un-crinkled
just enough to manage your hair- *like a lady*
No, this complex thin line of linage still evoluting,
trying to remain human all at once like ancestors did when
they locked muscles to fight and clenched teeth when "nègre"
first redeemed the shores

silly girl,
you can't control the wind

or the misconceptions of you

224W

four-dimensional roots twisted knotted
and the door is 10 steps too far
the outside months of layoff
have confined me to this building
and the air i breathe is up on
the slopes clogged
in the gutters
of putrid backed up sewers
in our hollow halls
the punching sounds of the man next door on his wife
-i hear them at night in the shower sometimes
when it echoes through the elevators

t.v. dinners have posted notes
monday-thru-friday sorting my life,
the fear of inevitable days
revenging lazy nights,
programmed t.v. channels
they know my favorites
welcoming me with open arms

the twisted beams of lights
hot cringes on skin
my couch now lumpy-bunched,
is conformed to my presence

Flashbacks

an adult daughter of an alcoholic
learning confessed words hidden for so long
memories that stood still until i breathed life, and remembered

fist-glories when i hugged my soul from going crazy
slipping self-hate notes, up nights,
i waited to ravel blankets twinned
lifting legs, cigarettes put-out

i married into what i ran away from
a man self-indulged that his good skipped out his fingertips
my wait shifted in times, calls ignored,
clapped into anger suffering bent on a man
that prefers to slumber in lullabies of beer bottles
making love to my body with his pores smelling like piss

i am broken, alluring tasting of salt drowning in his semen
but i love his battle when he tells his story- *listen*
he lays on turntables evoking chimes
my scent drenched in his hold, losing the voice of rehabilitation
naive to his bitter tongue drifting in unidentified dreams

my spirit opens, mellow, surrendered to my faith
i've thrown the Bible at him to many times
give it to God

my make of him-brought flashbacks of when i was a little girl
closing my eyes was the best thing to do, until bottoms up,
meant scared to death, so, i am waiting for him to notice me
pulling at my teeth, re-written into patient breezes.

Homemade

my grandfather's house has eyes
that stare
at me
remembering thickly coded chalk
outlining hopscotch squares
of little girls with lacey
white knee-highs

as little g.i. joes push and grind pedals
hard
humming
of big wheels
like trojan horses
racing in

distance

stored boxes
in the attic
full of toys
that breathe
under dust bunnies

the memories

photos rest against the wall
undone
famous family
posted up
wearing there brightest grins

we sit
on furniture
hardened yellow
plastic
that still remains
as a testimony of 3 generations
of the good ol' days
but
in a wooden box
kept in the attic
are the metals
of a proud young man

it's all
fading fast
red
now pink
awning
warped in time
waiting to be finished by
the hands that know its joints too well

Damning the Audience

My fingers creep in between my breast
pull open up this bony-cage
I fall short from being the demi-goddess
The one I always wanted to be
Prissy and full of power

like new-*used then tossed*-garbage

forget the way things were before the war
the hours I have talked and begged on one-knee
fate in the palms of those that haven't dreamed this hard
the peace I have found where my pen follows
the tranquility reappearing as a ghost
my voice raising into rage

I am screaming chained against the wall
got disheartening jones
Pulling me into oblivion
It tingles in my veins
Like hot gold-fire
I twinge

My end is the beginning
Of smog streets and dreams deferred
I make confessions of the soul
And sprinkle holy-terrific juice
I want you to hear my voice
full of disease hear these words and bind it
they embrace the end of my vertebrae
I gotta go

This lyrical diva is perplexed
And ashamed of craving a new reality

Status

i deserve a smack on my ass
to let me know I did the job well
early eggs over easy
bacon crispy
bagel lightly toasted butter with heavy cream cheese
orange juice barely to the rim
and finally to topped off, *your paper*
just how you like it at 7 a.m.

my layoff status is a weapon
to be your love slave
sweeping until my heart's content
manicured fingers soak in soapsuds
donna karen cornered
cashmere sweaters falling off hangers,
now inconstant wife damned
to be the intrigued object
a harrowing story gone wrong,
opened escaping into half asleep

Half Empty

married,
and after careful consideration

we wanted a baby

we begin making love every day,
counting 1-28 days 'Are you pregnant yet?'
'No' I respond and after 6 months no baby

my doctor gives me thermometers
and tells me to check my temperature

don't move,
don't wash we need an accurate graph of you
and when I call to make an appointment
they shift me to a non-important appointment,
because the ob/gyn only has certain days for the non-fertile clinic

He searches my womb scanning my body with metal objects

and I think when did baby making get so hard
I thought I would have a baby in the first year

And then loudly his voice echoes
remember he says,
'No deodorant soap, fragrances'
and in same breath

scoot your bottom down and

still wondering, by now I should have been rolling strollers

and staying up long nights,
doing double shifts with my husband
and watching my baby's first steps

but after two years no baby
my womb is still empty

Along the Banks of the Pymatuning

ma-ma
wants her
ashes scattered
along the banks of the Pymatuning
it is her wish
to be lost in the ripple of the tides
picked up by a rod cast out
tackled by the blue gill

my sister and i know
her gentle beauty
would not do well
buried in
a cozy condominium
not fit for a queen

we know
her spirit could not be settled in the breeze
on top of another lifeless shell
their color is not as
vivid as our ma-ma's

we will gasp her laughter
her soft touch
her memory
of a favorite t-shirt
in black to travel the waves
there is little earth room
to fit her passionate feisty soul
she will be sprinkled lightly savoring with memories

released into life
past into the winds
freeing the excerpts of her loved body
into different portions of life

Our Hips of Evolution

Our hips of evolution stops at rag doll-babies
birthing floated stories back to where our hips brushed,
existed, formulated to, cotton-jack breasts

our girdle sucks in the arrival of estrogen,
hug—hung on heavy hips…sway…sway
maybe it's the belly contracting spindles of
secret prayer visuals || learning one letter at a time

midwives pulling our mini life cycle
anxious hungry fingertips craving to know new ways
times before, where 15 windows shut
and back alleys were lotus flowers expanding

our hips of evolution can not be defined
in the form of fleshy cells cast over in battle dressings,
counting pulses
soaked in biscuits

only tipping scales to birth
maybe it's held on palms of tassels
tasks, babe on hip we walk
hung bent down so far

so how do you heal our cannel?

the pulsating scripts on water falls
latching on tilted wampams
soaked in crevices beyond panty liners
we are mummified in wounds still sore through roles

we are Picassas of evolution trotted
Painting the world with our toes
we heave all this, on our shoulders

Our hips of evolution,
Wrapped in genesis
Circular in clouds
Spacious bones collaborating
To cradle the heavenly,
cornbread-cupcakes served with a pot of greens
sweet potato pie on the traces of our thighs
we are eve's spawns
birth is the alpha spanned 360 degrees
breathing life on warmed ashes
modeling attitudes on metallic hips.

7 Breaths of Yearning

I sought miracles on rooftops
if only they could talk
shout out, *declare it*
take shape and claim their glory
my wounds were found before the war
but became marks when I could not
Find my testament

Healing is a lingering kiss
that lifts you from flesh
7 breaths of yearning
the closest to angel, i ever seen,
cradled in lullabies painted-dusky poses
my voice fractioned on rust metallic hinges
dropped to permanent portraits behind the wall
poised beginnings

sigh…

my soul has left my body, before
when streets lie empty
promises magnified to mossy mouths
become, the yeasted, on lifting grounds
forgotten bread to those that crave
i, a lady between two worlds
subtle in easy breezes

i push breath with mocha lips
Standing still, paused
Waiting for a sign, hello…*can you hear me?*

he answers, always ready knowing my
testament more than me, waves his magic
wand on constant waves of destiny
my sum full of regrets in omens standing,
if only I could remove the empty feelings

sigh...

when the crowd stopped looking
i was left feeling like a crumbled
piece of something pricked
half broken crossed-color restored in bellied faith
not realizing that reality was two inches from my nose
i am taking it in now, yesterdays
When i referred my self as third person
before the move-
that were too rotten to catch

Enough

There are broken pieces swept in dust pans
slapped against the side, ready to be thrown away
scattered on the kitchen floor, forcing my disappearance
I was ready to go after he added dents to the wall on the list
he didn't even care to wash this time
just stood on the stoop ready to drink his life away

my soul murdered by his empty words
running out my front door
i threw another bible just for keeps
just so he knew who my father was and maybe he could
get the devil off his back, maybe this time
he would come back and we could make love one last time

my mother always told me I would know when
I had enough, after he stole a jeep, after another
woman called, after he withdrew all my money out the bank
I would know when enough is enough
my trouble is that I don't want to give up
I carry my battle quiet in Saran Wrap
To mute the air-I left my legacy in a nightmare
still haunting, wanting to exist in this insanity

i am no longer whole, just a empty shell of torso walking
into another man's arms, he could love me better, but my soul
is still connected to my husband, our separation is an antique
precious on the jerks of kickstands I want more than dancing
through this madness, he now has a welcome is slippery,
he is the mass of dust, the suffocation
keeping me from my freedom

In Pittsburgh

IN PITTSBURGH

we stood erect
the sun smirking at our naïve postures
we, ran amuck and did not turn around
crying for a nation that if not had been victimize
would have eased out until the cries where silenced
making national announcements of remorse
these signs of the times broken into the mosh pit
we wave flags of heroism, wear armbands
close-pin flags that dangle
in unity,
we see the images that the world did not
censor in our own back yard.

IN PITTSBURGH

we sat on buses in fear
that downtown would no longer be there
tomorrow
we give quarters to
people with cell phones
asking drivers
are they scared to drive down Fifth?

IN PITTSBURGH

the younger people
smiled and cheered that
classes were cancelled,

no work today
time to sleep on couches,
eat out today
they ran
they stuck white crosses in the grassy moss
at soldiers and sailors hung flags half-staffed
IN PITTSBURGH

we will worry about this tomorrow
postpone our cries for the next couple hours
'til we know they aren't coming here
let us light candles on porches, silent one minute
from the noise that racks our brains
let the president worry about it tonight

IN PITTSBURGH

we kiss our children more
watch them do their homework
smile when they say innocent speech
and listen to the channels teach temporary psyche classes
TELL THEM THE TRUTH AMERICA
without hating Arabs and damning them
tell them that people hate, but we should love them
without revulsion to their god

Let us pray

IN PITTSBURGH

We hugged our skyline
Sent can goods to Somerset
And loved their spirits

But selfish of ourselves
We appreciated
Our blazing PPG and USX towers
Just a little bit more
Climbed on the thirteenth floor
And prayed for our future

Layered in History

it was my husband that taught me how to love
after so many men came in between lines
and spat on my spirit, sliced holes enough to
grab my soul with their movement
climbed inside my skin, and blended so well
shifting my armour into a thin plastic coat
giving me another easy breath

with him, we were a loveable chunk,
a metamorphous of what won't kill you,
can only make you pray harder
that's why when I lost his love somewhere
in transition in between the streets of Pittsburgh,
the affairs and late-night arrivals, cockfighting
to win him over, I pulled out a knife
and pinned it straight to my heart.

he sleeps under bridges now, while holding
my picture in one hand I am trying
to shed his reminders, peel of the dandruff
putting my life back on track
we are altered continuations, digging
for balance through romance memories
and wish-storms

our battle is visible but layered in history,
good bye to the one i love, our page turning
stories have been burning its fuel in the grave
for a long time.

we failed us

Heavenly

he knew it was time to go,
such little time on this cruel earth
the crowd grew still
as he stumbled with a wooden cross
two times his size
his side swollen and gauged from spears
that wounded his holy skin
and his beautiful face distorted from thorns
that punctured holes on his head
and the people that loved him
some cried
Jesus…Jesus

as their savior made his way to Calvary
each step
        each sin
           each tear
washed away
for the anger of man taking the weight of so much sin
to fold it into one line
Will you take him as your personal savior?

I would have like to be there has held the blind
      quiet as he walked on water
               silent as he took his last breath
inhaling his wondrous love

I would have pushed the people out the way to claim him
shouting and daring anyone

he allowed his body to be stretched as they hammered holes
in his hands bigger than then their heart
and as his head hung looking toward the heavens
'Why has thou forsaken me?'
the many stories, lectures yet come
will never come close to the pain Jesus felt
so heavenly
so beautifully
what he did for you and for me

Altar Call

Mary and I would be sharing the Alabaster Box
if I had a choice, stroking the helm of his cloak
his spirit flowing through kinetic vibes
her story prehistoric before I was ever
created out the dust, *a word spoken*

we are daughters of the arrival
marking our claims to the heavens
mopping up our destruction with
brillo pads, stains that have been
caressed with years of yearns and regrets
are flushed away--

Mary marked herself in history
with a blueprint in the Bible
her stones turned into anointed petals
cradled in the arch of her feet
we are one in the same
a trampled entrance with a door missing,
where there is an ending, *the beginning comes*
and the **X for exit turns into a cross**

last night in the altar call
my nanna led my mother and i
to the ending of the storm
all the curses washed away
we **three**, are different generations
women with stories that would make
your knees beg for mercy
now called to fulfill a purpose--

Printed in the United States
41542LVS00002B/470